Ancient Ballads and Songs Chiefly from Tradition, Manuscripts, and Scarce Works

Lyle, Thomas

bibliolife
old books. new life.

ANCIENT

BALLADS AND SONGS,

CHIEFLY

FROM TRADITION, MANUSCRIPTS,

AND SCARCE WORKS;

WITH

BIOGRAPHICAL AND ILLUSTRATIVE NOTICES,

INCLUDING

ORIGINAL POETRY.

By THOMAS LYLE.

LONDON:

PRINTED FOR L. RELFE, 13, CORNHILL;

WESTLEY AND TYRREL, DUBLIN; AND CONSTABLE AND CO.
EDINBURGH.

M.DCCC.XXVII.

PREFACE.

————

As opportunities presented, during the casual intervals of relaxation allowed the Editor from more immediate studies and pursuits, he has been wont to amuse himself, by gathering together, from various sources occasionally placed within his reach, the materials from which the three first sections of the present work have been arranged; and now, since these are about to be laid before the public, he hopes it will not be deemed over-presumptive upon his part, at this time to hazard the remark, that, were their respective merits to be estimated by the care and pains which have already been bestowed by him, in rendering them acceptable to a few admirers and patrons of this department of lyrical composition, his well-meant attempts to while away the tedium of an idle hour, with those who may not consider varieties such as the following, beneath their notice, will not then by him be deemed to have been futile, nor his bitherto labours to please them, abortive.

Reader, have you ever watched, or haply accompanied
the youth in his devious rambles through the glen, as,
in boyhood's dawning morn, he culled from the luxuriant
herbage, opening upon the fairy prospect around him, a
blossom of every hue that Flora garlands her Spring mantle
with? If so, you never will forget, while life's pulse
continues to vibrate warm within you, the glowing recollections which that lovely morning's perambulation hath
left behind it, upon memory's track. From the margin
of the still pool beneath the linn, the youthful enthusiast
gathers the white and the yellow water-lilies, leaving the
less inviting iris and the arrow-leafed water-plantain, to
preside over the blooming grot or dingle's recess, during
the absence of the fair nymphs of the burn; the rose-bay
willow, scarlet campion, and paler saxifrage, are anon gathered by him from the streamlet's dimpled margin; the
daffodil, golden-cup, and various coloured violets, perfuming and scentless, from the shelving bank above; while
the marshy mossy spot hollowed beneath the shadowing
mountain ash-tree, fringed over with heather-bell and poly-
pody, next afford him the light and the deep blooming
speckled orchis, the yellow asphodel, and the pink-eyed
sundew. Not yet satiated with young Summer's offerings,
the ambitious little urchin scales the summit of his elysium,
studded over with the changeful milk-wort, and adds to
his posie, the blue gentian, the eye-bright, the deep gold
and carmine streaked St. John's wort, and the Alpine

scorpion grass of etherial blue, with a golden star in its breast: so, having gathered his nosegay, and wreathed it round with a limber twig of meadow-sweet, or a tendril of woodbine, he returns home, and exultingly presents the treasure to his delighted parents, who forthwith are invited to rejoice with him in their turn, as he tells over, one by one, the various dyed blossoms, and enumerates the different localities of strath and fell, from whence he so lately collected them.

Time steals on apace, till life's meridian has settled over him; yet all the storms and vicissitudes with which fortune alternately has assailed his course, while journeying onward to this goal, cannot efface the sunny spots, which, of yore, kept hallowing and playing around his childhood's fancy, nor dim the pristine recollection which erst had called them forth into existence, and now matured them with manhood.

Even so, it fares with the legendary lore of Ballad and Song, which has been painted and impressed upon the young and susceptible mind, by the maiden, mother, or matron, who watched over our dawning years, while

" We danced our infancy upon their knees,"

which grew with our growth, and strengthened with our

strength, as our vivid imaginations continued straining to portray every trait of the mournful, warlike, or pathetic, into the fair semblance of reality—when our mind's eye saw them all before us dancing into life, beckoning our compassion, rousing us up to feats of chivalry, or entreating our tears! When each and all of these fancy-born hallucinations kept flitting before our excited mind by turns, until, wearied and exhausted, we had fallen asleep, and alternately dreamed them all over again.

But, drawing this digressive parallel to a close, regarding early virgin impressions, whether the same has been called into existence from the study of nature, garnished forth in her May-tide livery, or, rather, from the talismanic aspirations of song, seared down upon the plastic mind during the halcyon days of infancy, the Editor now submits to his reader, an outline of the little work before him, which, for arrangement's sake, he has divided into Four Sections.

The first of these Sections, embraces a few essays by Byrd, the celebrated pupil of Tallis, along with selections from the works of numerous other musicians and lyric composers of the sixteenth and seventeenth centuries. These lighter emanations of the muse of bygone times, the Editor doubts not, will be sufficiently appreciated by many; while, to others, who deem themselves passingly indifferent to every thing else which chimes not directly upon

"Some splendid passage in the last new poem,"

he would be inclined to remark, of these earlier Songs, what Burgh in his Anecdotes of Music, says of melody during the Elizabethian period, that those pieces, which, in their day, have afforded delight to the best judges of their respective merits, even now are entitled to examination as well as respect, however much the revolutions of taste and fashion may have diminished their popularity amongst us, their more polished and fastidious descendants. This First Section contains one hundred pieces, which, for the most part, are now only to be found sprinkled over the pages of a few rare or expensive works; and even these are occasionally placed beyond the reach of the majority of song admirers, while others of them, he hazards not to say, have long since been out of print, and remain altogether unknown, excepting to a very few antiquarians in lyrical lore.

The Second Section comprises a few excerpts from the unpublished minor poetry of Sir William Muir of Rowallan: the illustrative remarks upon the same, have been kindly furnished the Editor by the gentleman whose name is attached to the article; and by many, he doubts not,

this will be considered as the most interesting Section
of the work. It ever will remain the Editor's most
earnest wish, that the unpublished remains of this nearly
forgotten Scottish poet, should, at some time or other,
form a separate publication; and with the public, whose
will in these matters is often tantamount to a law, it now
rests to decide, whether or not this task should yet be
attempted by him. The Editor, after having transcribed
the whole of Sir William's recovered manuscript poetry,
with the exception of his psalmody, and read each specimen individually and repeatedly over, is inclined to say
much in favour of Rowallan's poetical powers, and even
wills to place this western baronet's abilities, as a candi-
date in the Parnassian scale, almost next in degree with
those of that much talked about, though little read or understood brother of the lyre, Sir William Drummond of
Hawthornden, who also was his contemporary. These
gentlemen having been born within nine years, and died
within eight years of each other, the former in the sixty-
third, and the latter in the sixty-fourth year, of their respective ages.

The Third Section, amongst other varieties, contains a
small portion of the Song and Ballad lore, that erst was
floating about on the wings of tradition, over the shires of
Renfrew and Ayr, during the era of the Editor's boyhood;
and which, some time ago, at passing intervals, were noted

down by him, partly from early recollections, and partly
from the singing of one or two individuals, whose memories
in these matters, had been greener than his own. These
reminiscences were generally committed by him to paper,
at the time, or soon afterwards, as nearly as the sets picked
up during his juvenile researches, warranted him to do;
and each traditionary specimen will now be found placed
in its respective class, along with some illustrative notice
or other, wherever the same has been deemed necessary.
These pieces, as various in merit, as in plot or incident,
are here given as they were found by him, so far as well
could be done, without unnecessarily trespassing beyond
the pale of decency and decorum; which restricting caveat,
he is sorry to acknowledge, has, in not a few instances,
caused him throw aside a number of superior pieces,
which, but for their freedom, might otherwise have been
admitted here, or any where else, as tolerably fair
specimens of lyrical composition in their own way; but
wherever, for the sake of introducing one or more of these,
he has altered, as seemed to him for the better, any relic
of the olden times, the correction, whatever it may be, is
acknowledged in its subjoined note—while the traditional
fragments gleaned by him, which now must be considered
as nearly if not altogether his own, when a whole could
not be procured, have been eked out a stanza or two, or
remodelled according to circumstances for the sake of
unity, and then embodied into a song, with the intent of

wresting from oblivion's grasp, some fine old and semi-forgotten melody, which he was anxious to see preserved, and equally tenacious that it should not be lost to posterity, if any trifling effort of his could avert the same.

The Fourth and last Section comprises a few of the Editor's own compositions.

Of the various and respectable individuals who have trodden over the same paths of Ancient Song he now regrettingly lingers upon, his limits here forbid him from saying any thing, as sufficient notices will be found within the body of the work, regarding all of them he has been necessitated to consult, while drawing up and arranging this little volume for the press.

Glasgow, 1st Sept. 1827.

SECTION I.

EARLY NATIONAL SONGS.

EARLY NATIONAL SONGS.

—————

WE commence our present specimens with the following "Sonets and Pastorales," excerpted from an elegantly printed 4to. work, in five parts, of which the following is the title:

"Psalmes, Sonets, and Songs of Sadnes and Pietie, made into musicke of five parts; whereof some of them going abroade among divers, in untrue coppies, are here truly corrected, and th' other being Songs very rare, and newly composed, are heere published for the recreation of all such as delight in Musicke; by WILLIAM BYRD, one of the Gent. of the Queen's Majestie's honorable Chappel. Printed by Thomas East, the Assigne of W. Byrd.—1588."

The work is dedicated to the Right Honourable Sir Christopher Hatton, Lord Chancellor of England, wherein the author states, that, at the desire of friends, and from the knowledge that many spurious copies of his Songs having got into public notice, he has been induced to publish the above, being his first printed work in English,

" To pass under your Lordship's favour and protection, hoping that by this occassion, these poor Songs of mine may happily yield some repose and recreation unto your Lordship's mind, &c." Byrd further states, that, should the present attempt be favourably received, " It shall encourage him to suffer some other things of more depth and skill to follow these, which being not yet finished, are of divers expected and desired."

In his epistle to the reader (who probably was also the reviewer of 1588), he modestly says, " In the expressing of these Songs, either by voices or instruments, if there happen to be any jar or dissonance, blame not the printer, who, I do assure thee, through his great pains and diligence, doth here deliver to thee a perfect and true copy. If, in the composition of these Songs, there be any fault by me committed, I desire the skilful either with courtesy to let the same be concealed, or in friendly sort to be thereof admonished, and at the next impression, he shall find the error reformed; remembering always, that it is more easy to find a fault, than to amend it."

Byrd was a musician of acknowledged merit and celebrity in his time, besides being an agreeable and respectable composer. One of his best known compositions at this day, perhaps, is " Non nobis Domini." He also was the author of several other musical works, published betwixt 1575 and 1618; for a list of which, see Burney, Hawkins, and Dr. Watt's Bibliotheca Britannica. Byrd died in 1623, aged eighty.

TO AMARILLIS.

Though Amarillis dance in green,
Like fairy queen, and sing full clear,
Corinna can with smiling cheer;
Yet since their eyes make hearts so sore,
   Hey-ho! chil [shall] love no more.

My sheep are lost for want of food,
And I so would, that all the day,
I sit and watch a herd-maid gay,
Who laughs to see me sigh so sore,
   Heigh-ho! chil love no more.

Her loving looks, her beauty bright,
Is such delight, that all in vain,
I love to like, and lose my gain,
For her that thanks me not therefore,
   Heigh-ho! chil love no move.

Ah wanton eyes, my friendly foes,
And cause of woes, your sweet desire,
Breeds flames of ice, and freeze in fire,
Ye scorn to see me weep so sore,
   Heigh-ho! chil love no more.

Love ye who list, I force him not,
Sith God it wot, the more I wail
The less my sighs and tears prevail;
What shall I do, but say therefore,
   Hey-ho! chil love no more.

CUPID'S SENTENCE.

Who likes to love, let him take heed,
 And wot you why?
Among the Gods it is decreed,
 That Love shall die;
And every wight that takes his part,
Shall forfeit each a mourning heart.

The cause of this as I have heard,
 A sort of dames,
Whose beauty he did not regard,
 Nor secret flames,
Complain'd before the Gods above,
That Gold corrupts the God of Love.

The Gods did storm to hear this news,
 And there they swore,
That sith he did such dames abuse
 He should no more
Be God of Love, but that he should
Both die and forfeit all his gold.

His bow and shafts they took away
 Before their eyes,
And gave these dames a longer day
 For to devise
Who should them keep, and they be bound
That love for gold should not be found.

These ladies striving long, at last
    They did agree
To give them to a maiden chast,
    Whom I did see;
Who with the same did pierce my breast:
Her beauty's rare, and so I rest.

MY MIND TO ME A KINGDOM IS.

My mind to me a kingdom is,
   Such perfect joy therein I find,
That it excels all other bliss
    That God or nature hath assign'd:
Though much I want that most would have,
Yet still my mind forbids to crave.

No princely port, nor wealthy store,
   No force to win a victory,
No wilie wit to salve a sore,
    No shape to win a loving eye;
To none of these I yield as thrall,
For why, my mind despise them all.

I see that plenty surfeits oft,
   And hasty climbers soonest fall;
I see that such as are aloft,
    Mishap doth threaten most of all;
These get with toil, and keep with fear:
Such cares my mind can never bear.

I press to bear no haughty sway,
  I wish no more than may suffice,
I do no more than well I may,
  Look what I want, my mind supplies;
Lo, thus I triumph like a king,
My mind's content with any thing.

I laugh not at another's loss,
  Nor grudge not at another's gain;
No worldly waves my mind can toss,
  I brook that is another's bane;
I fear no foe, nor fawn on friend,
I loathe not life, nor dread mine end.

My wealth is health and perfect ease,
  And conscience clear my chief defence,
I never seek by bribes to please,
  Nor by desert to give offence;
Thus do I live, thus will I die,
Would all do so as well as I!

WHERE FANCY FOND.

WHERE fancy fond for pleasure pleads,
  And reason keeps poor hope in jail,
There time it is to take my beads,
  And pray that beauty may prevail;
Or else despair will win the field
Where reason, hope, and pleasure yield.

My eyes presume to judge this case,
   Whose judgment reason doth disdain,
But beauty with her wanton face,
   Stands to defend the case, is plain;
And at the bar of sweet delight,
She pleads that fancy must be right.

But shame will not have reason yield,
   Though grief do swear it shall be so,
As though it were a perfect shield
   To blush and fear to tell my woe,
Where silence forces will at last
To wish for wit, when hope is past.

So far hath fond desire outrun
   The bond which reason set out first,
That where delight the fray begun,
   I would now say, if that I durst,
That in her stead ten thousand woes
Have sprung in field where pleasure grows.

Oh that I might declare the rest
   Of all the toys which fancy turns,
Like towers of wind within my breast
   Where fire is hid, that never burns;
Then should I try one of the twain,
Either to love, or to disdain.

But fine conceit dares not declare
   The strange conflict of hope and fear,
Lest reason should be left so bare
   That love durst whisper in mine ear,

And tell me how my fancy shall
Bring reason to be beauty's thrall.

I must therefore with silence build
  The labyrinth of my delight,
Till love hath tried in open field
  Which of the twain shall win the fight;
I fear me reason must give place,
If fancy fond win beauty's grace.

IF WOMEN COULD BE FAIR.

If women could be fair and never fond,
  Or that their beauty might continue still,
I would not marvel though they made men bond
  By service long to purchase their good will;
But when I see how frail these creatures are,
I laugh that men forget themselves so far.

To mark what choice they make, and how they change,
  How, leaving best, the worst they choose out still,
And how, like haggards, wild about they range,
  Scorning after reason to follow will;
Who would not shake such buzzards from the fist,
And let them fly, fair fools, what way they list?

Yet for our sport, we fawn and flatter both,
  To pass the time when nothing else can please,
And train them on to yield by subtle oath,
  The sweet content that gives such humour ease;
And then we say, when we their follies try,
To play with fools, oh, what a fool was I!

WHAT PLEASURE HAVE GREAT PRINCES.

WHAT pleasure have great princes,
    More dainty to their choice,
Than herdmen wild, who, careless,
    In quiet life rejoice,
And fortune's fate not fearing,
Sing sweet in summer morning?

Their dealings plain and rightful,
    Are void of all deceit;
They never know how spiteful
    It is to kneel and wait
On favourite presumptuous,
Whose pride is vain and sumptuous.

All day their flocks each tendeth,
    At night they take their rest
More quiet than he who sendeth
    His ship into the east,
Where gold and pearl are plenty,
But getting very dainty.

For lawyers and their pleading
    They 'steem it not a straw,
They think that honest meaning
    Is of itself a law,
Where conscience judgeth plainly;
They spend no money vainly.

Oh, happy who thus liveth,
   Not caring much for gold,
With clothing which sufficeth
   To keep him from the cold;
Though poor and plain his diet,
Yet merry it is, and quiet.

IN FIELDS ABROAD.

In fields abroad, where trumpets shrill do sound,
   Where glaves and shields do give and take the knocks,
Where bodies dead do overspread the ground,
   And friends to foes, are common butchers' blocks,
A gallant shot, well managing his piece,
In my conceit, deserves a golden fleece.

Amid the seas, a gallant ship set out,
   Wherein nor men, nor yet munition lacks,
In greatest winds that spareth not a clout,
   But cuts the waves in spite of weather's wracks;
Would force a swain that comes of cowards' kind,
To change himself, and be of noble mind.

Who makes his seat a stately stamping steed,
   Whose neighs and plays are princely to behold,
Whose courage stout, whose eyes are fiery red,
   Whose joints well knit, whose harness all of gold,
Doth well deserve to be no meaner thing,
Than Persian knight, whose horse made him a king.

FAREWELL, FALSE LOVE.

FAREWELL, false love, the oracle of lies,
　A mortal foe, and enemy to rest;
An envious boy, from whom all cares arise;
　A bastard vile, a beast with rage possess'd;
A way of error, a temple full of treason,
　In all effects contrary unto reason.

A poison'd serpent, cover'd all with flowers,
　Mother of sighs, and murtherer of repose;
A sea of sorrows, whence are drawn such showers
　As moisture lends to every grief that grows;
A school of guile, a net of deep deceit,
A gilded hook that holds a poison'd bait;

A fortress foil'd, which reason did defend;
　A syren song, a fever of the mind;
A maze wherein affection finds no end;
　A raging cloud that runs before the wind;
A substance like the shadow of the sun;
A goal of grief for which the wisest run;

A quenchless fire, a nurse of trembling fear;
　A path that leads to peril and mishap;
A true retreat of sorrow and despair;
　An idle boy that sleeps in pleasure's lap;
A deep mistrust of that which certain seems;
A hope of that which reason doubtful deems.

c

ALL AS A SEA.

ALL as a sea the world no other is,
　　Ourselves are ships still tossed to and fro;
And lo, each man his love to that or this,
　　Is like a storm to drive the ship to go;
That thus our life in doubt of shipwreck stands,
Our will's the rock, our want of skill the sands.

Our passions be the pirates still that spoil,
　　And overboard cast out our reason's freight;
The mariners that day and night do toil,
　　Be our conceits that do on pleasure wait;
Pleasure, master, doth tyrannise the ship,
And giveth virtue secretly the nip.

The compass is a mind to compass all,
　　Both pleasure, profit, place, and fame, for nought;
The winds that blow, men overweening call;
　　The merchandise is wit full dearly bought;
Trial the anchor cast upon experience,
For labour, life, and all ado the recompence.

WHEN AUTUMN RIPES.

When autumn ripes the fruitful fields of grain,
  And Ceres doth in all her pomp appear,
The heavy ear doth break the stalk in twain,
  Whereby we see this by experience clear,
Her own excess doth cause her proper spoil,
  And make her corn to rot upon the soil.

So worldly wealth and great abundance, mars
  That sharpness of our senses and our wits,
And oftentimes our understanding bars,
  And dulls the same with many careful fits;
Then since excess procures our spoil and pain,
The mean prefer before immoderate gain.

OF FLATTERING SPEECH BEWARE.

Of flattering speech, with sugar'd words, beware;
  Suspect the heart whose face doth fawn and smile;
With trusting these, the world is clogg'd with care,
  And few there be can 'scape these vipers vile;
With pleasing speech they promise and protest,
When careful hearts lie hid within their breast.

The faithful wight, doth need no colours brave;
  But those that trust in time his truth shall try,
Where fawning mates cannot their credit save,
  Without a cloak to flatter, feign, and lie;
No foe so fell, nor yet so hard to 'scape,
As is the foe that fawns with friendly shape.

J. H. M.

The two foregoing Pieces are from "A Choice of Emblems
and other Devices," &c. selected by Geffrey Whitney—1586.

FLORA GAVE ME FAIREST FLOWERS.

Flora gave me fairest flowers,
    None so fair in Flora's treasure;
These I placed on Phillis' bowers,
    She was pleased, and she my pleasure:
Smiling meadows seem to say,
Come ye wantons here to play.

Wilbye—1598.

CONTENT.

There is a jewel which no Indian mines can buy,
    No chemic art can counterfeit;
It makes men rich in greatest poverty;
    Makes water wine, turns wooden cups to gold,
    The homely whistle to sweet music's strain;
Seldom it comes, to few from heaven sent,
That much in little, all in naught—Content.

Wilbye—1609.

TO SHORTEN WINTER'S SADNESS.

To shorten winter's sadness,
See where the nymphs with gladness,
Disguised all are coming,
Right wantonly a-mumming.

Whilst youthful sports are lasting,
To feasting turn our fasting;
With revels and with wassals,
Make grief and care our vassals.

For youth it well beseemeth,
That pleasure he esteemeth;
And sullen age is hated,
That mirth would have abated.

The above is from " Ballets and Madrigals to five voyces, by
THOMAS WEELKES, Organist of the College of Winchester."—
Lond. 1598.　4to. Este.

IN PRIDE OF MAY.

IN pride of May, the fields are gay,
　The birds do sweetly sing;
So nature would, that all things should,
　With joy begin the spring.

Then Lady dear, do you appear
　In beauty like the spring;
I will dare say, the birds that day
　More cheerfully will sing.

　　　　　　　　　　WEELKES—1598.

COLD WINTER'S ICE IS FLED.

COLD winter's ice is fled and gone,
　And summer brags on every tree;
The red-breast peeps amidst the throng
　Of wood-born birds, that wanton be;
Each one forgets what they have been,
And so doth Phillis, summer's queen.

　　　　　　　　　　WEELKES—1600.

WHY ARE YOU, LADIES, STAYING.

WHY are you, Ladies, staying,
And your Lords gone a-Maying?
Run apace and meet them,
And with your garlands greet them;
'Twere pity they should miss you,
For they will sweetly kiss you!

Hark! hark! I hear the dancing,
And a nimble morris prancing;
The bagpipe and the morris-bells,
That they are not far hence us tells;
Come let us all go thither,
And dance like friends together.

WEELKES—1600.

THE WINE THAT I SO DEARLY GOT.

THE wine that I so dearly got,
Sweetly sipping, mine eyes hath blear'd;
And the more I am barr'd the pot,
The more to drink my thirst is steer'd;
But since thereby my heart is cheer'd,
Maugre ill luck, and spiteful slanders,
Mine eyes shall not be my commanders;
For I maintain, and ever shall,
Better the windows hide the dangers,
Than to spoil both the house and all.

From Madrigalles to 5 and 6 voices; translated out of sundrie
Italian authors.—Yonge, London: 1597.   4to. Este.

THERE IS A GARDEN IN HER FACE.

THERE is a garden in her face,
　Where roses and white lilies grow;
A heavenly paradise is that place,
　Wherein all pleasant fruits do grow;
There cherries grow that none may buy,
Till cherry-ripe themselves do cry.

Those cherries fairly do inclose
　Of orient pearl a double row,
Which when her lovely laughter shows,
　They look like rose-buds fill'd with snow;
Yet them no peer nor prince may buy,
Till cherry-ripe themselves do cry.

Her eyes like angels watch them still;
　Her brows like bended bows do stand,
Threatening with piercing frowns to kill
　All that approach with eye or hand
These sacred cherries to come nigh,
Till cherry-ripe themselves do cry.

O HEAVY HEART.

O heavy heart, what harms are hid,
　Thy help is hurt, thy hap is hard;
If thou shouldst break, as God forbid,
　Then should desert want his reward:
Hope well to have, hate not sweet thought,
Foul cruel storms fair calms have brought;

After sharp showers the sun shines fair,
Hope comes likewise after despair.

In hope, a king doth go to war;
   In hope, a lover lives full long;
In hope, a merchant sails full far;
   In hope, just men do suffer wrong;
In hope, the ploughman sows his seed;
Thus hope helps thousands at their need:
Then faint not heart, among the rest,
Whatever chance, hope thou the best.

Though wit bids will blow the retreat,
   Will cannot work as wit would wish;
When that the roach doth taste the bait,
   Too late to warn the hungry fish;
When cities burn on fiery flame,
Great rivers scarce may quench the same;
If will and fancy be agreed,
Too late for wit to bid take heed.

But yet it seems a foolish drift,
   To follow will and leave the wit;
The wanton horse that runs too swift,
   May well be stay'd upon the bit;
But check a horse amid his race,
And out of doubt you mar his pace;
Though wit and reason doth men teach
Never to climb above their reach.

The two foregoing Pieces are from " An Houre's Recreation
in Musicke, by RICH. ALISON."—1606.

SEPHESTIA'S SONG TO HER CHILD,

AFTER ESCAPING FROM SHIPWRECK.

MOTHER'S wag, pretty boy,
Father's sorrow, father's joy,
When thy father first did see
Such a boy by him and me,
He was glad, I was woe,
Fortune changed made him so;
When he had left his pretty boy,
Last his sorrow, first his joy.
Weep not my wanton, smile upon my knee;
When thou art old, there's grief enough for thee.

The wanton smiled, father wept,
Mother cried, baby leap'd;
More he crow'd, more he cried,
Nature could not sorrow hide,
He must go, he must kiss
Child and mother, baby bless;
For he left his pretty boy,
Father's sorrow, father's joy.
Weep not my wanton, smile upon my knee;
When thou art old, there's grief enough for thee.

The above beautiful stanzas are from the Arcadia of ROBERT
GREEN. Lond. 1616. Green was born a gentleman, but com-
pelled from necessity to support himself and his family by the
efforts of his pen. His publications are from forty-five to fifty
in number, from the sale of which he had managed to obtain a
precarious livelihood. He died about the year 1592.

TO COLIN CLOUT.

BEAUTY sat bathing by a spring,
　　Where fairest shades did hide her,
The winds blew calm, the birds did sing,
　　The cool streams ran beside her;
My wanton thoughts enticed mine eye
　　To see what was forbidden;
But better memory said, fie,
　　So vain desire was chidden:
　　　　Hey nonnie, nonnie, &c.

Into a slumber then I fell,
　　When fond imagination
Seem'd to see, but could not tell
　　Her feature or her fashion;
But even as babes in dreams do smile,
　　And sometimes fall a-weeping;
So I awak'd as wise this while,
　　As when I fell a-sleeping:
　　　　Hey nonnie, nonnie, &c.

The above is Song 13th in "England's Helicon," 1600; Lond.
4to. p. 192. This scarce and valuable work contains 150 separate
Songs and Poems, contributed by the different literary characters
of the day, or selected from contemporary works of acknowledged
merit.

WHO PROSTRATE LIES AT WOMAN'S FEET.

WHO prostrate lies at woman's feet,
And calls them darlings dear and sweet,

Protesting love, and craving grace,
And praising oft a foolish face,
Are oftentimes deceived at last;
They catch at naught, and hold it fast.

BATESON—1604.

WHEN FIRST MINE EYES.

WHEN first mine eyes did view and mark
   Thy beauty fair for to behold;
And when my ears 'gan first to hark
   The pleasant words that thou me told,
I would as then I had been as free
From ears to hear, and eyes to see.

And when in mind I did consent
   To follow thus my fancy's will,
And when my heart did first relent
   To wist such bait myself to spill,
I would my heart had been as thine,
Or else thy heart as soft as mine.

O flatterer false! thou traitor born,
   What mischief more might thou devise,
Than thy dear friend to have in scorn,
   And him to wound in sundry-wise,
Which still a friend pretends to be,
And art not so, by proof I see;
Fie, fie upon such treachery!

The above Lyric is by HUNNIS, one of the contributors to the
" Paradise of Dainty Divices," in the time of Edward IV. and
Mary; author of " A Hive of Honey," "A Hive of Honeysuckle,"
a translation of the Psalms, &c. Hunnis died in the year 1568.

THE NYMPHS TO THEIR MAY QUEEN.

WITH fragrant flowers we strew the way,
And make this our chief holiday;
For though this clime was bless'd of yore,
Yet was it never proud before:
  O beauteous Queen of second Troy,
  Accept of our unfeigned joy.

Now the air is sweeter than sweet balm,
And satyrs dance about the palm;
Now earth with verdure newly dight,
Gives perfect signs of her delight:
  O beauteous Queen of second Troy,
  Accept of our unfeigned joy.

Now birds record new harmony,
And trees do whistle melody,
And every thing that nature breeds
Doth clad itself in pleasant weeds:
  O beauteous Queen of second Troy,
  Accept of our unfeigned joy.

The above is by THOMAS WATSON, whose poetical works are numerous, and of various merit. Stephens prefers his Sonnets to those of Shakespeare. He was born in 1560, and died in 1592.

TAKE ALL ADVENTURES PATIENTLY.

THOUGH pinching be a privy pain,
To want's desire, that is but vain;
Though some be curs'd, and some be kind,
Subdue the worst with patient mind.

Who sits so high, who sits so low,
Who feels such joy, that feels no woe?
When bale is bad, good boot is nigh,
Take all adventures patiently.

To marry a sheep, to marry a shrew,
To meet with a friend, to meet with a foe,
Those checks of chance can no man fly,
But God himself that rules the sky.

From the Play of "Tom Tyler and his Wife," 1598; in Garrick's Scarce Plays.

A NYMPH'S DISDAIN OF LOVE.

HEY down a down, did Dian sing,
    Amongst her virgins sitting,
Than love there is no vainer thing
    For maidens most unfitting;
        And so think I,
    With a down, down derry.

When women knew no woe,
    But lived themselves to please,
Man's feigning guiles they did not know,
    The ground of their disease.

Unborn was false suspect;
    No thought of jealousy;
From wanton toys, and fond affect,
    The virgin's life was free.

D

At length men used charms,
 To which, what maids gave ear,
Embracing gladly endless harms,
 Anon enthralled were.

Thus women welcom'd woe,
 Disguis'd in name of love;
A jealous hell, a painted show,
 So shall they find that prove.

Hey down a down, did Dian sing,
 Amongst her virgins sitting,
Than love there is no vainer thing,
 For maidens most unfitting.

DULCINA.

As at noon Dulcina rested
 In her sweet and shady bower,
Came a shepherd and requested
 In her lap to sleep an hour;
But from her looks a wound he took,
 So deep, that for a further boon
The nymph he prays; whereto she says,
 Forego me now, come to me soon!

But in vain she did conjure him
 To depart her presence so,
Having a thousand tongues to allure him,
 And but one to bid him go;

When lips invite, and eyes delight,
   And cheeks as fresh as rose in June,
Persuade delay, what boots to say,
   Forego me now, come to me soon!

But what promise or profession
   From his hands could purchase scope?
.Who would sell the sweet possession
   Of such beauty for a hope!
Or for the sight of lingering night,
   Forego the present joys of noon,
Though ne'er so fair her speeches were,
   Forego me now, come to me soon!

SHALL I, LIKE A HERMIT.

SHALL I, like a hermit, dwell
On a rock or in a cell,
Calling home the smallest part
That is missing of my heart,
To bestow it, where I may
 · Meet a rival every day?
   If she undervalues me,
   What care I how fair she be.

Were her tresses angel gold;
If a stranger may be bold,
Unrebuked, unafraid,
To convert them to a braid,

And, with little more ado,
Work them into bracelets too;
　If the mine be grown so free,
　What care I how rich it be.

Were her hands as rich a prize
As her hairs or precious eyes;
If she lay them out to take
Kisses for good manners' sake;
And let every lover skip
From her hand unto her lip;
　If she seem not chaste to me,
　What care I how chaste she be.

No, she must be perfect snow,
In effect as well as show,
Warming but as snow-balls do,
Not like fire by burning too;
But when she by chance hath got
To her heart a second lot,
　Then, if others share with me,
　Farewell her, whate'er she be.

The three foregoing Ballads are by SIR WALTER RALEIGH, whose chequered and eventful life is too well known, to require in this place, any comments of ours. His poetical works, although the meanest of his literary productions, are pure and classical; while his lyrics, were they generally known, would merit insertion in any collection. He was born at Haye's Farm in Devonshire, in 1552; and died upon the scaffold in 1618. See his "Last Hours," by D'Israeli.

WHENCE COMES MY LOVE.

WHENCE comes my love? O heart disclose!
It was from cheeks that shamed the rose,
From lips that spoil'd the ruby's praise,
From eyes that mock'd the diamond's blaze:
   Whence came my woes? as freely own;
   Ah me! 'twas from a heart like stone.

The blushing cheek speaks modest mind,
The lips befitting words most kind,
The eye does tempt to love's desire,
And seems to say, 'Tis Cupid's fire;
   Yet all so fair, bespeak my moan,
   Sith nought doth say, the heart of stone.

Why thus my love, so kind, bespeak
Sweet lip, sweet eye, sweet blushing cheek,
Yet not a heart to save my pain;
O Venus! take thy gifts again;
   Make not so fair, to cause our moan,
   Or make a heart that's like our own.

The above is "A Sonnet made on Isabella Markham, when I first thought her fair, as she stood at the Princess's window, in goodly attire, and talked to divers in the Court-yard," from a M. S. of JOHN HARRINGTON'S, dated 1564, and inserted into the Nugæ Antiquæ. This John Harrington, Esq. says Ellis, was father to the above mentioned Sir John. In the reign of Queen Mary, he was imprisoned for having espoused the cause of Elizabeth, who rewarded his attention, by the reversion of a grant of lands at Kelston, near Bath. He was born in 1534, and died in 1582. His love verses, says Campbell, possess an elegance and terseness more modern by a hundred years, than others of his contemporaries.

ROSALIND'S MADRIGAL.

LOVE in my bosom, like a bee,
   Doth suck his sweet,
Now with his wings he plays with me,
   Now with his feet;
Within mine eyes he makes his nest,
His bed amidst my tender breast,
My kisses are his daily feast,
And yet he robs me of my rest:
   Ah! wanton, will ye!

And if I sleep, then pierceth he
   With pretty slight,
And makes his pillow of my knee,
   The live long night;
Strike I the lute, he tunes the string;
He music plays, if I but sing;
He lends me every lovely thing—
Yet cruel, he my heart doth sting:
   Ah! wanton, will ye!

Else I, with roses every day,
   Will whip you hence;
And bind ye when ye long to play,
   For your offence;
I'll shut my eyes to keep you in,
I'll make you fast it for your sin,
I'll count your power not worth a pin—
Helas! what hereby shall I win,
   If he gainsay me!

What if I beat the wanton boy,
  With many a rod?
He will repay me with annoy,
  Because a god!
Then sit thou softly on my knee,
And let thy bower my bosom be;
Lurk in mine eyes, I like of thee,
O Cupid! so thou pity me!
  Spare not, but play thee.

The above Ballad is by DR. THOMAS LODGE. His plays and
poetry possess considerable merit. He was born in 1556, and
died in 1625.

WHAT BIRD SO SINGS.

WHAT bird so sings, yet so does wail?
'Tis Philomel, the nightingale;
Jugg, jugg, jugg, jugg, terue, she cries,
And hailing earth, to heaven she flies.—Cuckoo!
Ha, ha, hark, hark, the cuckoos sing
Cuckoo, to welcome in the spring.

Brave prick song, who is't now we hear?
'Tis the lark's silver leer-a-leer;
Chirup, the sparrow, flies away,
For he fell to't ere break of day:
Ha, ha, hark, hark, the cuckoos sing
Cuckoo, to welcome in the spring.

CUPID AND CAMPASPE.

Cupid and my Campaspe play'd
At cards for kisses; Cupid paid:
He stakes his quiver, bow, and arrows,
His mother's doves, and team of sparrows,
Loses them too; then down he throws
The coral of his lip, the rose
Growing on's cheek (but none knows how),
With these, the crystal of his brow,
And then the dimple of his chin:
All these did my Campaspe win.
At last he set her both his eyes,
She won, and Cupid blind did rise:
O Love! has she done this to thee?
What shall, alas! become of me?

The two foregoing Sonnets are the composition of John Lyly, a celebrated writer in the time of Queen Elizabeth, born about 1553, in the wilds of Kent. He was the author of nine plays, and several lyrics, published betwixt 1580 and 1632, which, along with the above, certainly merit preservation. The last of these, " Cupid and Campaspe," is to be found in his play of " Alexander and Campaspe," printed in 1591. The time of this author's death is uncertain, but Ellis fixes it about the year 1600.

THE MAD MAID'S SONG.

Good-morrow to the day so fair,
  Good-morrow, Sir, to you;
Good-morrow to mine own torn hair,
  Bedabbled all with dew.

Good-morrow to this primrose too;
    Good-morning to each maid,
That will with flowers the tomb bestrew
    Wherein my love is laid.

Ah, woe is me, woe, woe is me,
    Alack and well-a-day!
For pity, Sir, find out that bee
    Which bore my love away.

I'll seek him in your bonnet brave,
    I'll seek him in your eyes;
Nay, now I think they've made his grave
    In the bed of strawberries.

I'll seek him there, I know ere this,
    The cold, cold earth doth shake him;
But I will go, or send a kiss
    By you, Sir, to awake him.

Pray, hurt him not; though he be dead,
    He knows well who do love him,
And who with green turfs rear his head,
    And who so rudely move him.

He's soft and tender, pray take heed,
    With bands of cowslips bind him,
And bring him home; but 'tis decreed
    That I shall never find him.

NIGHT SONG TO JULIA.

HER lamp the glow-worm lend me,
The shooting stars attend me,
And the elves also, whose little eyes glow
Like the sparks of fire befriend me.

No will-o'-the-wisp beslight thee,
Nor snake, or slow-worm bite thee,
But on, on thy way, nor lingering stay,
Since ghost there is none to affright thee.

Then let not the darkness thee cumber,
What though the moon does slumber,
The stars of the night will lend thee their light,
Like tapers clear without number.

Then, Julia, let me woo thee,
Thus, thus to come unto me,
And when I shall meet thy silvery feet,
My soul I will pour into thee.

CHERRY-RIPE.

CHERRY-ripe, ripe, ripe I cry,
Full and fair ones, come and buy!
If so be you ask me where
They do grow, I answer there,

Where my Julia's lips do smile;
There's the land, or cherry isle;
Whose plantations fully show
All the year where cherries grow.

The three foregoing Songs are by ROBERT HERRICK, who appears to have been a poet of very considerable merit. Within these few years, his memory has been happily revived by Drake, Irvin, Campbell, Retrospective Review, &c. all of whom, attracted by the native sweetness and harmony of his versification, have drawn largely upon his writings. Herrick's poetry is considerable, and he may be placed at the head of the minor poets of his time. He lived to an advanced age, and was born in London in 1591. He published a volume of his poetry, under the title of "Hesperides." 1648. 8vo.

DETRACTION'S REWARD.

WHO seeks to tame the blustering wind,
    Or cause the floods bend to his will,
Or else against dame nature's kind
    To change things fram'd by cunning skill:
That man I think bestoweth pain,
Though that his labour be in vain.

Who strives to break the sturdy steel,
    Or goeth about to stay the sun;
Who thinks to cause an oak to reel,
    Which never can by force be done:
That man likewise bestoweth pain,
Though that his labour be in vain.

So he likewise, that goes about
   To please each eye and every ear,
Had need to have without a doubt
   A golden gift with him to bear;
For evil report shall be his gain,
Though he bestow both toil and pain.

Copied, by Percy, from an old M. S. in the Cotton Library,
[Vesp. A. 25.] entitled, " Divers things of Henry VIII.'s time."

THE CUCKOO.

SUMMER is a-coming in;
   Loud sings the cuckoo;
Groweth seed, and bloweth mead,
   And springeth the wood now:
      Sing cuckoo!
Ewe bleateth after lamb;
   Loweth after calf the cow;
Bullock starteth, the buck verteth,
   Merrily sings cuckoo:
      Cuckoo! cuckoo!
Well singest thou, cuckoo!
Ne swik thu naver nu.

The above descriptive piece is said by Ritson to be the most
ancient English song now extant; and is preserved in the Har-
leian Library in M. S.　It is supposed to have been composed in
the thirteenth century, in Henry the Third's time.　The orthography is here modernised.　Our authority translates the last
line, by rendering it, " Mayest thou never cease."

THOMAS MORLEY was Bachelor in Music, and gentleman of Queen Elizabeth's Royal Chapel. He published
several books of Madrigals and Ballads, betwixt the years
1593 and 1600, besides " A plaine and easy Introduction
to Pracktical Musick, in form of a Dialogue;" Lond. 1597
—1608, fol.; reprinted again, *totidem verbis*, by Randel,
under the inspection of Dr. Howard, about the year 1780.
For more than a century, this remained a standard work,
and was the companion of every musical amateur. We
even find a writer in the Monthly Review for 1785, vol.
72, page 581, stating this to be the most ample and lu-
minous general treatise upon practical music and composition, they could boast of possessing at that time.

" Madrigals," says the writer of the article Music, for
Brewster's Encyclopedia, " commenced about the middle
of the sixteenth century. These were vocal compositions
in many parts, generally in fugæ; they do not seem to
have contributed greatly to the improvement of melody;
but, as greater freedom of combination and modulation
was allowed than in the church, these secular compositions
afforded an opportunity to ingenious men, of trying new
effects, by which the bounds of harmony were enlarged."
" Morley, and all the old writers upon modern music,
before the use of bars, affixed no other meaning to the
MODES, or MOODS as they were then called, than that of
regulators of time or measure."

The following eight Madrigals are selected from a slim
4to. in five parts, with neatly engraven frontispiece, containing twenty-one pieces in all, of which this is the title,
"Quintus, Tenor, &c. of Thomas Morley, The First Booke
of Balletts to Five Voyces. In London, by Thomas Este,
1595."

DAINTY, FINE, SWEET NYMPH.

DAINTY, fine, sweet nymph, delightful,
While the sun aloft is mounting,
Sit we here, our loves recounting, Fa, la, la,
With sugar'd glosses, among these roses.

Why, alas! are you so spiteful,
Dainty nymph, but, oh! too cruel?
Wilt thou kill thy dearest jewel? Fa, la, la,
Kill then and bliss me, but first come kiss me.

NOW IS THE MONTH OF MAYING.

Now is the month of Maying,
When merry lads are playing
Each with his bonny lass
Upon the greeny grass.

The spring clad all in gladness
Doth laugh at winter's sadness,
And to the bagpipe's sound
The nymphs tread out their ground.

Fie, then, why sit we musing,
Youth's sweet delight refusing;
Say, dainty nymphs, and speak,
Shall we play barley-break? [1]

SHOOT, FALSE LOVE.

SHOOT, false love, I care not,
Spend thy shafts, and spare not;
I fear not I thy might,
And less I way thy spight.

All naked I unarm me,
If thou canst, now shoot and harm me;
So lightly I esteem thee,
As now a child I deem thee.

Long thy bow did fear me,
While thy pomp did blear me;
But now I do perceive
Thy art is to deceive.

And every simple lover
All thy falsehood can discover;
Then weep love, and be sorry,
For thou hast lost thy glory.

---

[1] This Song will also be found in the Aberdeen Cantus. The pastime
of Barley-break, is here alluded to, as well as in Song 14 of the same
Collection, "Come love, let's walk in yonder spring." In the west of
Scotland, this pastime is still common amongst children.

SING WE AND CHANT IT.

Sing we, and chant it,
While love doth grant it;
Not long youth lasteth,
And old age hasteth,
Now is best leisure
To take our pleasure.

All things invite us,
Now to delight us;
Hence care be packing,
No mirth be lacking;
Let's spare no treasure,
To live in pleasure.

MY BONNY LASS, SHE SMILETH.

My bonny lass, she smileth,
When she my heart beguileth;
Smile less, dear love, therefore,
And you shall love me more.

When she her sweet eye turneth,
Oh, how my heart it burneth!
Dear love, call in their light,
Or else you burn me quite.

I SAW MY LOVELY PHILLIS.

I saw my lovely Phillis
    Laid on a bank of lilies,
But when herself alone she there espieth,
On me she smileth, and home away she flieth.

    Why flies my best beloved,
    From me her love approved?
See, see what I have here, fine sweet musk roses,
To deck that bosom, where love herself reposes.

WHAT SAITH MY DAINTY DARLING.

What saith my dainty darling,
    Shall I now your love obtain?
Long time I sued for grace,
    And grace you granted me,
When time shall serve and place,
    Can any fitter be?

This crystal running fountain,
    In his language, saith, come love!
The birds, the trees, the fields,
    Else none can us behold;
This bank soft lying yields,
    And saith, nice fools, be bold.

YOU THAT WONT TO MY PIPES SOUND.

You that wont to my pipes sound,
　　Daintily to tread your ground;
Jolly shepherds, and nymphs sweet, lirum, lirum,
Under the weather, hand in hand uniting,
The lovely god come greet: lirum, lirum.

Lo! triumphing, brave comes he,
　　All in pomp and majesty,
Monarch of the world and king; lirum, lirum,
Let who so list him, dare to resist him,
We our voice uniting, of his high acts will sing: &c.

MAY NEVER WAS THE MONTH OF LOVE.

May never was the month of love,
　　For May is full of flowers;
But rather April wet by kind,
　　For love is full of showers.

With soothing words, enthralling souls,
　　She chains in servile bands!
Her eye in silence hath a speech,
　　Which eye best understands.

Her little sweet hath many sours,
　　Short hap, immortal harms;
Her loving looks are murdering darts,
　　Her songs, bewitching charms.

Like winter rose, and summer ice,
    Her joys are still untimely;
Before her, hope—behind, remorse,
    Fair first, in fine, unseemly.

Plough not the seas, sow not the sands,
    Leave off your idle pain;
Seek other mistress for your mind,
    Love's service is in vain.

LOSS IN DELAYS.

Shun delays, they breed remorse,
    Take thy time, while time is lent thee;
Creeping snails have weakest force,
    Fly their fault, least thou repent thee:
Good is best when soonest wrought,
Lingering labour comes to nought.

Hoist up sail, while gale doth lost,
    Tide and wind stay no man's pleasure;
Seek not time when time is past,
    Sober speed is wisdom's leisure:
After-wits are dearly bought,
Let thy fore-wit guide thy thought.

Time wears all his locks before,
    Take thou hold upon his forehead;
When he flies he turns no more,
    And behind, his scalp is naked:

Works adjourn'd have many stays,
Long demurs breed new delays.

Seek thy salve while sore is green,
   Fester'd wounds ask deeper lancing;
After-cures are seldom seen,
   Often sought, scarce ever chancing:
Time and place give best advice,
Out of season, out of price.

The two foregoing Ballads are by ROBERT SOUTHWELL, a very
superior, though voluminous and religious, poet, in the reign of
Elizabeth. He was born in 1562; and, upon the 21st February,
1595 or 1596, he was hanged and quartered at Tyburn for his ad-
herence to Jesuitical principles. It is remarkable, says Ellis, that
the few copies of his works which are now known to exist, are
the remnants of at least twenty-four different editions, of which
eleven were printed betwixt 1593 and 1600.

THE GENTLE SEASON OF THE YEAR.

THE gentle season of the year
Hath made my blooming branch appear,
   And beautified the land with flowers;
The air doth savour with delight,
The heavens do smile to see the sight,
   And yet mine eyes augment their showers.

The meads are mantled all with green,
The trembling leaves have cloth'd the treen,
   The birds, with feathers new, do sing;

But I, poor soul, whom wrong doth rack,
Attire myself in mourning black,
   Whose leaf doth fall amidst his spring.

And as you see the scarlet rose,
In her sweet prime, her sweets disclose,
   Whose hue is with the sun reviv'd;
So in the April of mine age,
My lively colours do assuage,
   Because my sunshine is deprived.

My heart that wonted was, of yore,
Light as the winds abroad to soar,
   Amongst the buds, when beauty springs,
Now only hovers over you,
As doth the bird that's taken anew,
   And mourns when all her neighbours sing.

When every man is bent to sport,
Then pensive I alone resort
   Into some solitary walk,
As doth the doleful turtle dove,
Who, having lost her faithful love,
   Sits mourning on some wither'd stalk.

Then to myself I do recount,
How far my woes my joys surmount,
   How love requiteth me with hate;
How all my pleasures end in pain,
How hate doth say my hope is vain,
   How fortune frowns upon my state.

And in this mood, charg'd with despair,
With vapour'd sighs I dim the air,
    And to the gods make this request—
That, by the ending of my life,
I may have truce with this strange strife,
    And bring my soul to better rest.

From the " Phœnix Nest," edition 1593.

THE DAWN OF LOVE.

THE dew drops that at first of day
    Hangs on the violet flower,
Although it shimmereth in the ray,
    And trembleth at the zephyr's power,
Shows not so fair and pleasantly
As love that bursts from beauty's eye.

The little bird that clear doth sing
    In shelter of green trees,
When flowerets sweet begin to spring
    In dew bespangled mees,
Is not so pleasant to mine ear
As love that scantly speaks for fear.

The rose when first it doth prepare
    Its ruddy leaves to spread,
And kissed by the cold night air,
    Hangs down its coyen head,

Is not so fair as love that speaks
In unbid blush on beauty's cheeks.

The pains of war when streams of blood
   Are smoking on the ground;
When foemen brim of lustihood,
   All mix'd in death are found;
Yea death itself is lightlier borne,
Than cruel beauty's smiling scorn.

From the old scarce pastoral poem of " The Shepheardes' Garland," printed by Jaggard, 1597.

COME AWAY, COME SWEET LOVE.

COME away, come sweet love!
   The golden morning breaks;
All the earth, all the air,
   Of love and pleasure speaks;
Teach thine arms then to embrace,
   And sweet rosy lips to kiss,
   And mix our souls in mutual bliss:
Eyes were made for beauty's grace,
   Viewing, ruing, love's long pain,
   Procur'd by beauty's long disdain.

Come away, come sweet love!
   The golden morning wastes;
While the sun, from his sphere
   His fiery arrows casts,

Making all the shadows fly,
 Playing, staying in the grove,
 To entertain the stealth of love:
Thither, sweet love, let us hie,
 Flying, dying in desire,
 Wing'd with sweet hopes, and heavenly fire.

Come away, come sweet love!
 Do not in vain adorn
Beauty's grace, that should arise
 Like to the naked morn;
Lilies on the river side,
 And fair Cyprian flowers newly born,
 Ask no beauties but their own:
Ornament is nurse of pride,
 Flying, dying in desire,
 Wing'd with sweet hopes, and heavenly pride.

The foregoing song is from " England's Helicon." In a manuscript collection of airs in our possession, written above two hundred years ago, the music of the above song is to be found, taken, we presume, either from " England's Helicon," or the same source from whence it had been originally obtained.

HER TRIUMPH.

See the chariot at hand here of love,
 Wherein my lady rideth!
Each that draws is a swan or a dove,
 And well the car love guideth.

As she goes, all hearts do duty
    Unto her beauty;
And enamour'd do wish, so they might
    But enjoy such a sight,
That they still were to run by her side,
Thro' swords, thro' seas, whither she would ride.

Do but look on her eyes, they do light
    All that love's world compriseth!
Do but look on her, it is bright
    As love's star when it riseth!
Do but mark, her forehead's smoother
    Than words that soothe her!
And from her arch'd brows, such a grace
    Sheds itself through the face,
As alone there triumphs to the life
All the gain, all the good of the elements' strife.

Have you seen but a bright lily grow,
    Before rude hands have touch'd it?
Have you mark'd but the fall of the snow,
    Before the soil hath smutch'd it?
Have you felt the wool of the beaver,
    Or swan's down ever?
Or have smell'd of the bud o' the briar?
    Or the 'nard in the fire?
Or have tasted the bag of the bee?
O so white! O so soft! O so sweet is she!

F

THE SWEET NEGLECT.

STILL to be neat, still to be dress'd,
As you were going to a feast;
Still to be powder'd, still perfum'd;
Lady! it is to be presum'd,
Though art's hid causes are not found,
All is not sweet, all is not sound.

Give me a look, give me a face,
That makes simplicity a grace;
Robes loosely flowing, hair as free:
Such sweet neglect more taketh me,
Than all the adulteries of art;
They strike mine eyes, but not my heart.

The two foregoing Pieces are by BEN JOHNSON, the friend and contemporary of Shakespeare. The last is from his " Silent Woman," first acted in 1609. He was born 1574, died 1657.

———————————

WOMAN'S INCONSTANCY.

I lov'd thee once, I'll love no more,
 Thine be the grief, as is the blame;
Thou art not what thou wast before,
 What reason I should be the same?
He that can love, unlov'd again,
Hath better store of love than brain;
God send me love my debts to pay,
While unthrifts fool their love away.

Nothing could have my love o'erthrown,
   If thou hadst still continued mine;
Yea, if thou hadst remain'd thy own,
' I might perchance have yet been thine;
But thou thy freedom did recal,
That, if thou might, elsewhere enthral;
And then how could I but disdain
A captive's captive to remain!

When new desires had conquer'd thee,
   And chang'd the object of thy will;
It had been lethargy in me,
   Not constancy, to love thee still;
Yea, it had been a sin to go
And prostitute affection so;
Since we are taught no prayers to say,
To such as must to others pray.

Yet do thou glory in thy choice,—
   Thy choice, of his good fortune boast;
I'll neither grieve nor yet rejoice
   To see him gain what I have lost:
The height of my disdain shall be,
To laugh at him, to blush for thee,
To love thee still, but go no more
A-begging at a beggar's door.

The author of the above Sonnet, SIR ROBERT AYTON, in 1606, says Pinkerton, wrote some Latin poems in the Deliciæ Poetarum Scotarum, and some light genteel pieces in English, two of which are published in Select Scottish Ballads, vol. I. One or two more may be found in a collection of Scottish Poems by Watson the

printer, published, according to Alexander Campbell, editor of
Albyn's Anthology, in 1706–9–11–12.   Ayton was Private Secretary to Queen Anne of Denmark, wife of James the Sixth; he
is little known as a poet, but the present specimen must induce a
regret that he had not written more—it rivals even the Sonnets
of Drummond in elegance of fancy and harmony of versification.

THE JOLLY ALE-DRINKER.

I cannot eat but little meat,
   My stomach is not good;
But sure I think, that I can drink
   With him that wears a hood:
Though I go bare, take ye no care,
   I nothing am a cold.
I stuff my skin so full within,
   With jolly good ale and old.
Back and sides go bare, go bare,
   Both foot and hand go cold;
But belly, God send thee good ale enough,
   Whether it be new or old.

I love no roast, but a nut brown toast,
   And a crab laid on the fire;
A little bread shall serve my stead,
   For much I not desire,
No frost or snow, no wind I know,
   Can hurt me if I would:
I am so wrapp'd, and thoroughly lapp'd
   With jolly good.ale and old.
Back and sides go, &c.

And Tib my wife, that as her life,
    Loveth good ale to seek;
Full oft drinks she, till you may see
    The tears run down her cheek.
Then doth she trowl to me the bowl,
    Even as a malt-woman should;
And faith, sweet-heart, I took my part
    Of this jolly good ale and old.
Back and sides go, &c.

The above Bacchanalian Piece is by Dr. JOHN STILL, born at Grantham, in Lincolnshire, about 1542. After passing through several gradations in the church, and having been successively Master of St. John's and Trinity Colleges, and Vice-Chancellor of Cambridge, he attained the mitre at Bath and Wells, after the demise of Bishop Godwin, and died in 1607.

Some curious notices regarding Dr. Still, will be found in the Nugæ Antiquæ, contained in a Letter from John Harrington to Prince Henry, wherein are several strong delineations of the simple humour and genius of these times.

Bishop Still was author of the earliest English drama, that exhibited any approaches to regular comedy, " Gamer Gurton's Needle," acted in 1566, though not printed until 1575, in which " the Jolly Ale-Drinkers" first appeared. Our copy of the Ballad is taken from " Poor Robin's Almanack," for 1708, on the left hand side of this eccentric compiler's column for April.

THE CHOICE.

SHE that denies me, I would have;
    Who craves me, I despise;
Venus hath power to rule mine heart,
    But not to please mine eyes:

Temptations offer'd I still scorn,
  Denied, I cling them still;
I'll neither glut mine appetite,
  Nor seek to starve my will.

Diana doubly clothed, offends;
  So Venus, naked quite:
The last begets a surfeit, and
  The other no delight.
That crafty girl shall please me best,
  That no for yea can say,
And every wanton willing kiss,
  Can season with a nay.

GIVE MY LOVE GOOD-MORROW.

PACK clouds away, and welcome day,
  With night we banish sorrow;
Sweet air blow soft, mount lark aloft,
  To give my love good-morrow:
Wings from the wind, to please her mind,
  Notes from the lark I'll borrow;
Bird prune thy wing, nightingale sing,
  To give my love good-morrow;
To give my love good-morrow,
Notes from them all I'll borrow.

Wake from thy nest, robin red-breast,
  Sing, birds, in every furrow;
And from each bill let music shrill,
  Give my fair love good-morrow;

Blackbird and thrush, in every bush,
 Stare, linnet, and cock-sparrow,
You pretty elves, amongst yourselves,
 Sing my fair love good-morrow;
To give my love good-morrow,
Sing birds in every furrow.

The above sprightly Sonnets are from the " Rape of Lucrece,"
1608, by THOMAS HEYWOOD, the time of whose birth and death
are alike unknown. He was an actor, and had more traffic with
the stage than any man who ever lived, if we except the Spanish
author, Lope de Vega. Heywood must indeed have been a man
of prodigious industry, having, besides numerous other works, and
attending to his business as an actor, had either, as is stated in the
preface to his " English Traveller," an entire hand, or at least a
main finger, in 220 plays, published betwixt 1596 and 1640; so
say the learned editors of the " Old English Drama," while Ellis
in his " Specimens" reduces their number to 120. Of this great
number of plays, no more than 23 have come down to us, besides
nine others which are doubtfully attributed to him. His Songs
are scattered over his remaining plays, and are of various merit.

LOVERS' FOLLIES.

If love be life, I long to die,
 Live they that list for me:
And he that gains the most thereby,
 A fool at least shall be.
But he that feels the sorest fits,
'Scapes with no less than loss of wits:
 Unhappy life they gain,
 Which love do entertain.

In day by fained looks they live,
　By lying dreams by night;
Each frown a deadly wound doth give,
　Each smile a false delight;
If 't hap the lady pleasant seem,
It is for others' love they deem;
　　If void she seem of joy,
　　Disdain doth make her coy.

Such is the peace that lovers find,
　Such is the life they lead;
Blown here and there with every wind,
　Like flowers in the mead;
Now war, now peace, now war again,
Desire, despair, delight, disdain;
　　Though dead, in midst of life;
　　In peace, and yet at strife.

By FRANCIS DAVIDSON, son of William Davidson, secretary to
Queen Elizabeth, who suffered so much through that princess's
caprice and cruelty in the tragical affair of Mary Queen of Scots.

LOVE LOVETH MOST IN SECRET.

THE fountains smoke, and yet no flames they show,
　Stars shine all night, though undiscern'd by day;
The trees do spring, yet are not seen to grow,
　And shadows move, although they seem to stay;
In winter's woe, is buried summer's bliss,
And love loves most when love most secret is.

The stillest streams descry the greatest deep,
    The clearest sky is subject to a shower;
Conceit's most sweet, whereas it seems to sleep,
    And fairest days do in the morning lower;
The silent groves, sweet nymphs they cannot miss,
For love loves most when love most secret is.

The rarest jewels hidden virtue yield,
    The sweet of traffic is a secret gain;
The year once old doth show a barren field,
    And plants seem dead, and yet they spring again;
Cupid is blind,—the reason why, is this,
Love loveth most, when love most secret is.

From Jones' " Garden of Delights," 1600.

SWEET DAY SO COOL.

SWEET day so cool, so calm, so bright,
    The bridal of the earth and sky;
The dew shall weep thy fall to-night,
    For thou must die.

Sweet rose, whose hue, angry and brave,
    Bids the rash gazer wipe his eye;
Thy root is ever in its grave,
    And thou must die.

Only a sweet and virtuous soul,
    Like season'd timber, never gives;
But though the whole world turn to coal,
    Then chiefly lives.

By GEORGE HERBERT, born 1593, died 1632 or 1633.

THOMAS RAVENSCROFT, B. M. was an eminent English
Musician and Publisher, who flourished betwixt the years
1600 and 1635.

Besides the Melismata, about to be noticed, Ravenscroft
was author of " A brief Discourse of the true but neglected
use of characterizing the degrees by their perfection and
diminution, in measurable music, against the common
practice and custom of the times," London, 1614, 4to.
He also edited and composed the best collection of Psalm
Tunes, which, till then, had appeared in England, in four
parts, published in 1621–23, 8vo.   This book contains a
melody for every one of the hundred and fifty Psalms,
many of them by the editor himself.

The following varieties are selected from a beautiful
single 4to. volume, the same size with that of Byrd and
Morley, containing twenty-three separate pieces with
music, in parts, entitled, " Melismata, Mvsicall Phansies,
fitting the Covrt, Citie, and Covntrey hvmovrs, to three,
four, and five voyces:
      To all delightfull, except to the spitefull,
      To none offensiue, except to the pensiue.
London, printed by William Stansby for Thomas Adams,
1611."

The work is preceded by two dedications, the first of
which is addressed to " the Right worshippfull, the true

favourers of Musicke and all vertue, Mr. Thomas Ravenscroft and Mr. William Ravenscroft, Esquires, to whom
he subscribes himself their affectionate kinseman, T. R."
The second dedication is a general one, being addressed
" To the noblest of the Court, liberallest of the Countrey,
and freest of the Citie," wherein he states, " that, being
little or much beholden to some of each rank [in select-
ing materials for this work], I study and strive to please
you in your own elements."

The most of the pieces contained in the " Melismata,"
may be ascribed to a much older date than the time of
Ravenscroft. We believe that this worthy musician has
availed himself, by culling a few lays here and there, as
best suited his purpose, from the floating song literature of
the day, thereby diversifying and rendering more valuable
his selection than it otherwise would have been, had he
composed the poetry for his airs, as Byrd and a few others
about this period seem to have done.

THE COURTIER'S GOOD-MORROW TO HIS MISTRESS,
FROM COURT VARIETIES.

CANST thou love and lie alone?
    Love is so disgraced!
Pleasure is best wherein is rest
    In a heart embraced.
      Rise, rise, rise,
Daylight do not burn out,
    Bells do ring and birds do sing,
Only I that mourn out.

Morning star doth now appear,
Wind is hush'd, and sky is clear;
Come, come away, come, come away,
Canst thou love and burn out day?
       Rise, rise, rise, &c.

THE CROWNING OF BELPHEBE.

Now flowers your odours breathe,
    And all the air perfume;
Grow in this honour'd wreath,
    And with no storms consume.

Hail, hail, and welcome her,
    Thou glory of our green;
Receive this flowery sphere,
    And be the shepherd's queen.

Oh kneel, and do her homage now,
    That calls our hearts like fate;
Now rise, your humble bosoms bow,
    And lead her to her state.

MERCURY'S SONG, THE MESSENGER OF THE GODS.

HASTE, haste, post-haste, make haste, and away,
The tide tarrieth no man, it makes no delay;
Trudge, trudge, for thy life, for virtue must fly,
These journeys are rife with thee, poor Mercury.

SERVANTS OUT OF SERVICE
ARE GOING TO THE CITY TO LOOK FOR NEW.

HEIGH-HO, away the mare,
Let us set aside all care;
If any man be dispos'd to try,
Lo, here comes a lusty crew,
That are enforc'd to cry, a new master, a new!
Hey now, we'll take small pains,
And yet we'll thrive, hey now;
We neither mind to beg nor starve,
We will have more than we deserve,
We'll cut their throats that are alive.

THE YOUNG NURSE'S REQUEST.
FROM CITY ROUNDS.

I pray you, good mother, give me leave
To play with little John,
To make his bed, and comb his head,
And come again anon.
Or else beat me as you think good,
For I love John alone.

THE PAINTER'S SONG OF LONDON.
FROM CITY CONCEITS.

WHERE are you, fair maids, that have need of our trades?
I'll sell you a rare confection;
Will you have your faces spread, either with white or red;
Will you buy any fair complexion?

G

My drugs are no dregs, for I have whites of eggs,
 Made in a rare confection,
Red leather and surflet water, scarlet colour or staves-aker;
 Will you buy any fair complexion?

A BELLMAN'S SONG.

MAIDS to bed, and cover coal,
Let the mouse out of her hole;
Crickets, crickets in the chimney sing,
Whilst the little bell doth ring,
If fast asleep, who can tell
When the clapper hits the bell.

THE THREE RAVENS.
FROM COUNTRY PASTIMES.

THERE were three ravens sat on a tree,
 Down a down, hey down;
There were three ravens sat on a tree,
 With a down;
There were three ravens sat on a tree,
They were as black as they might be,
 With a down, derry, derry, derry, down, down.

The one of them said to his mate,
Where shall we our breakfast take?

Down in yonder green field,
There lies a knight slain under his shield.

His hounds they lie down at his feet,
So well they can their master keep.

His hawks they fly so eagerly,
There's no fowl dare him come nigh.

Down there comes a fallow doe,
As great with young as she might go;

She lifted up his bloody head,
And kiss'd his wounds that were so red;

She got him up upon her back,
And carried him to earthen lake;

She buried him before the prime;
She was dead herself ere even-song time.

God send every gentleman
Such hawks, such hounds, and such a leman.

From internal evidence, the "Three Ravens" appears to have been an old Ballad when Ravenscroft introduced it into his "Melismata," written, perhaps, in or about the reign of Henry the Eighth. He has passed over the history of this rich and sublimely wild production, as other collators of his period were wont to do, consequently, we remain ignorant of the circumstance which erst called forth its composition. The "Two Ravens," although poetical and descriptive, is evidently a more recent composition, built upon the former; we subjoin this version in illustration of what we now have stated.

THE TWO RAVENS.

There were two ravens sat on a tree,
Large and black, as black may be;

And one unto the other 'gan say,
Where shall we go and dine to-day?
Shall we go dine by the wild salt sea?
Shall we go dine 'neath the greenwood tree?

As I sat on the deep sea sand,
I saw a fair ship nigh at land,
I waved my wings, I bent my beak,
The ship sunk, and I heard a shriek;
There they lie, one, two, and three,
I shall dine by the wild salt sea.

Come, I will show ye a sweeter sight,
A lonesome glen, and a new-slain knight;
His blood yet on the grass is hot,
His sword half-drawn, his shafts unshot;
And no one kens that he lies there,
But his hawk, his hound, and his lady fair.

His hound is to the hunting gane,
His hawk to fetch the wild fowl hame,
His lady's away with another mate,
So we shall make our dinner sweet;
Our dinner's sure, our feasting free,
Come, and dine by the greenwood tree.

Ye shall sit on his white hause-bane,
I will pike out his bonnie blue een;
Ye'll take a tress of his yellow hair,
To theak your nest when it grows bare;
The gowden down on his young chin,
Will do to sewe my young ones in.

Oh! cauld and bare will his bed be,
When winter storms sing in the tree;
At his head a turf, at his feet a stone,
He will sleep, nor hear the maiden's moan;
O'er his white bones the birds shall fly,
The wild deer bound, and foxes cry.

The late Mr. John Findlay, author of Wallace, or the Vale of Ellerslie, &c. seems also to have borne Ravenscroft's " Three Ravens" in mind, when he composed his Dirge of the Slain Knight, beginning,

> " A knight there came from the field of slain,
> His steed was drench'd with the falling rain."

THE MARRIAGE OF THE FROGGIE AND THE MOUSE.

FROM COUNTRY PASTIMES.

IT was the froggie in the well,
  Humble dum, humble dum;
And the merry mouse in the mill,
  Tweedle, tweedle, twino.

The froggie would a-wooing ride,
Sword and buckler by his side.

When he was upon his high horse set,
His boots they shone as black as jet.

When he came to the merry mill-pin,
Ho! mistress mouse, be ye within.

She cries, out o'er the seedy mill-dam,
O yes, kind Sir, and that I am.

And then came out the dusty mouse,
Saying, ' I am lady of this house.'

Hast thou any mind of me?
I have e'en great mind of thee.

Then he pull'd out a farthing fine,
Away, and fetch us bread and wine.

The table where they both did dine,
Was all clad o'er with bread and wine.

And who shall this marriage make?
Who but our lord, which is the rat.

What shall we have to our supper?
Three beans in a pound of butter.

And now when supper they were at,
The frog, the mouse, and even the rat.

Then came in sly Gib, our cat,
And catch'd the mouse even by the back.

This made them all to separate;
And the frog leap'd on the floor so flat.

Then came in gobble Dick, our drake,
And drew the frog even to the lake.

Our lord the rat ran up the wall,
A goodly company, the devil go with all!

The above Ballad is collated with another copy noted down from recitation. This may have been a satire of the olden times, but against what or whom, it is now immaterial to know, or perhaps a nursery chant. The modern Ballad, " Rowley would a wooing go," is a happy imitation of the foregoing.

A WOOING SONG OF A YEOMAN OF KENT'S SON.

FROM COUNTRY PASTIMES.

I have house and land in Kent,
    And if you'll love me, love me now;
Twopence-halfpenny is my rent,
    I cannot come every day to woo.
      Twopence-halfpenny is his rent,
      He cannot come every day to woo.

I am my father's eldest son,
    My mother eke doth love me well;
For I can bravely clout my shoon,
    And I full well can ring a bell.
      For he can bravely, &c.

My father he gave me a hog,
    My mother she gave me a sow;
I have a god-father dwells thereby,
    And he on me bestow'd a plough.
      He has a god-father, &c.

One time, I gave thee a paper of pins,
    Another time, a tawdry lace;
And if thou wilt not grant me love,
    In truth I'll die before thy face.
      And if thou wilt not, &c.

I have been twice our Whitsun lord,
    I have had ladies many fair,
And eke thou hast my heart in hold,
    And in my mind seems passing rare.
      And eke thou hast, &c.

I will put on my best white slope,
　　And I will wear my yellow hose,
And on my head a good gray hat,
　　And in it I'll stick a lovely rose.
　　　　And on his head, &c.

Wherefore, cease off, make no delay,
　　And if you'll love me, love me now;
Or else I'll seek some other where,
　　For I cannot come every day to woo.
　　　Or else he'll seek some other where,
　　　For he cannot come every day to woo.

　　We are inclined to hazard a conjecture, that the above " Wooing Song" is the parent stem of our goodly Scottish piece, " I hae
laid a herring in saut;" and that the air of the latter has been
altered a little by some skilful hand from that of the Wooing Song,
and now is by every one called a standard Scottish tune, when in
reality it is an English one, as any amateur may satisfy himself,
by running over the bars of the one after the other, in Song 22,
of the " Melismata;" even the Songs, in some points, bearing a
resemblance, independent of the terminal lines of the first and
concluding stanzas of the English set of words.　We never have
seen that old Scottish Ballad alluded to by Lord Hales, in notes
to his Selections from the Bannatyne M.S. which seems to be the
primary Scottish version of the same; but those who have, may
compare the twain, and see how far they resemble each other.
One stanza quoted by his Lordship is the following:

　　" I ha a wie lairdschip down in the Merse,
　　　[Lass an ye loe me, tell me now,]
　　The nynetenth pairt of a gusse's gerse,
　　　And I wo' na cum every day to wow."

THE PRETTY PET.

A blythe and bonnie country lass,
 Heigh-ho, bonnie lass,
Sat sighing on the tender grass,
 And weeping said, Will none come woo me?
A smicker boy, a lither swain,
 Heigh-ho, lither swain,
That in his love was wanton fain,
 With smiling looks came straight unto her.

When as the wanton wench espied,
 Heigh-ho, when she espied,
The means to make herself a bride,
 She simper'd smooth as bonny bell;
The swain that saw her squint-e'ed kind,
 Heigh-ho, squint-e'ed kind,
His arms about her body twined,
 And, Fair lass, how fare ye? Well.

The country kit said, well forsooth,
 Heigh-ho, well forsooth,
But that I have a longing tooth,
 A longing tooth that makes me cry.
Alas, said he, what gars thy grief,
 Heigh-ho, what gars thy grief?
A wound, quoth she, without relief,
 I fear a maid that I must die.

If that be all, the shepherd said,
 Heigh-ho, shepherd said,
He makes thee wife it, gentle maid,
 And so secure thy malady;

Hereon they kiss'd with many an oath,
   Heigh-ho with many an oath;
And 'fore god Pan did plight their troth,
   And to the church did hie them fast.

And God send every pretty pet,
   Heigh-ho, the pretty pet,
That fears to die of this conceit,
   So kind a friend to help at last.

                              BECKLER—1621.

PHILLIDA AND CORYDON.

In the merry month of May,
In a morn by break of day,
Forth I walk'd the wood so wide,
When as May was in her pride,
There I spied, all alone,
Phillida and Corydon.

Much ado there was, God wot!
He would love, and she would not:
She said, never man was true:
He said, none was false to you;
He said, he had lov'd her long:
She said, love should have no wrong.

Corydon would kiss her then,
She said, maids must kiss no men,

Till they did for good and all.
Then she made the shepherd call
All the heavens to witness truth:
Never lov'd a truer youth.

Thus, with many a pretty oath,
Yea and nay, and faith and troth!
Such as silly shepherds use,
When they will not love abuse;
Love, which had been long deluded,
Was with kisses sweet concluded:
 And Phillida, with garlands gay,
 Was crown'd the lady of the May.

PHILLIS THE FAIR.

On a hill there grows a flower,
 Fair befall the dainty sweet!
By that flower, there is a bower
 Where the heavenly muses meet.

In that bower there is a chair,
 Fringed all about with gold,
Where doth sit the fairest fair
 That ever eye did yet behold;—

It is Phillis, fair and bright;
 She that is the shepherd's joy;
She that Venus did despite,
 And did blind her little boy.

Who would not that face admire!
  Who would not this saint adore!
Who would not this sight desire,
  Though he thought to see no more!

Thou that art the shepherds' queen,
  Look upon thy love-sick swain;
By thy comfort, have been seen
  Dead men brought to life again.

The two foregoing Pieces are the composition of NICHOLAS BRETON, whose poety is considerable, and of various merit; an imperfect copy of the former of these, together with his " Go, muse, rock me asleep," have been inserted by Percy into the third vol. of " Reliques," without his knowing who their author was. Playford, in his " Introduction to the Skill of Musick," 1665, quotes the first stanza of Phillida and Corydon, set to music, for two voices, with the attached signature, B. R.   Nicholas Breton supplied the press with a rich diversity of ingenious compositions, for more than forty years.   He was born in 1555; died, 1624.

ANNE HATHAWAY.

WOULD you be taught, ye feather'd throng,
With love's sweet notes to grace your song,
To pierce the heart with thrilling lay,
Listen to mine Anne Hathaway!
She hath a way to sing so clear,
Phœbus might wondering stop to hear;

To melt the sad, make blithe the gay,
And nature charm, Anne hath a way;
    She hath a way,
     Anne Hathaway,
To breathe delight, Anne hath a way.

When envy's breath, and rancorous tooth,
Do soil and bite fair worth and truth,
And merit to distress betray,
To soothe the heart, Anne hath a way;
She hath a way to chase despair;
To heal all grief, to soothe all care,
Turn foulest night to fairest day,
Thou knowest, fond heart, Anne hath a way;
    She hath a way,
     Anne Hathaway;
To make grief bliss, Anne hath a way.

But were it to my fancy given,
To rate her charms, I'd call them heaven,
For though a mortal made of clay,
Angels must love Anne Hathaway;
She hath a way, so to controul,
To rapture the imprison'd soul,
And sweetest heaven on earth display,
That to be heaven, Anne hath a way;
    She hath a way,
     Anne Hathaway;
To be heaven's self, Anne hath a way.

The above is doubtfully ascribed to SHAKESPEARE, and purports
to have been addressed to the lady he married: " To the idol of

H

mine eyes, and the delight of mine heart, Anne Hathaway."
This lady was eight years older than Shakespeare, but still only
in her twenty-sixth year, when he married her—"an age," says
Dr. Drake, "compatible with youth, and with the most alluring
beauty."

WHY SO PALE.

Why so pale and wan, fond lover?
　　Prethee, why so pale?
Will, when looking well, can't move her;
　　Looking ill, prevail?
　　Prethee, why so pale?

Why so dull and mute, young sinner?
　　Prethee, why so mute?
Will, when speaking well, can't win her;
　　Saying nothing, doe't?
　　Prethee, why so mute?

Quit, for shame! this will not move,
　　This cannot take her;
If of herself she will not love,
　　Nothing can make her:
　　The devil take her!

By Sir John Suckling. This sprightly knight was born in
1613. He spoke Latin at five years of age, and wrote it when
nine. He possessed a general knowledge of polite literature; but
applied himself more particularly to music and poetry. In the

course of his foreign travels, he made a campaign under Gustavus Adolphus; and after his return, raised a splendid troop of horse at the expense of twelve thousand pounds, for the service of the king (Lloyd's Memoirs). This troop, with Sir John at its head, behaved so ill in their engagement with the Scots upon the English border, in 1639, as to occasion the famous lampoon by Sir John Mennis, " Sir John he got him an ambling nag, &c." (Percy, II. 323,) which was set to an Irish tune, and much sung by the parliamentarians.

This disastrous expedition, says Nichols, and the ridicule that attended it, was supposed to have hastened his death, which happened in 1641, in the twenty-eighth or twenty-ninth year of his age. The whole of his works were published several times by Tonson, and in two neat volumes by Davis, in 1770.

HE THAT LOVES A ROSY CHEEK.

He that loves a rosy cheek,
　　Or a coral lip admires,
Or from star-like eyes doth seek
　　Fuel to maintain his fires;
As old time makes these decay,
So his flames must waste away.

But a smooth and steadfast mind,
　　Gentle thoughts, and calm desires,
Hearts with equal love combin'd,
　　Kindle never-dying fires;
Where these are not, I despise
Lovely cheeks, or lips, or eyes.

No tears, Celia, now shall win
　My resolv'd heart to return;
I have search'd thy soul within,
　And find nought but pride and scorn;
I have learn'd thy arts, and now
Can disdain as much as thou:
　Some power, in my revenge, convey
　That love to her I cast away.

ASK ME NO MORE.

Ask me no more,—where Jove bestows,
When June is past, the fading rose;
For in your beauty's orient deep,
These flowers as in their causes sleep.

Ask me no more,—whither do stray
The golden atoms of the day;
For in pure love heaven did prepare
Those powders to enrich your hair.

Ask me no more,—whither doth haste
The nightingale, when May is past;
For in your sweet dividing throat
She winters, and keeps warm her note.

Ask me no more,—where those stars light
That downwards fall in dead of night;
For in your eyes they sit, and there
Fixed become, as in their sphere.

Ask me no more,—if east or west
The phœnix builds her spicy nest;
For unto you, at last she flies,
And in your fragrant bosom dies.

GOOD COUNSEL TO A YOUNG MAID.

When you the sun-burn'd pilgrim see,
   Fainting with thirst, haste to the springs;
Mark how at first, with bended knee,
   He courts the crystal nymph, and flings
His body to the earth, and he,
Prostrate adores the flowing deity.

But when his sweaty face is drench'd
   In her cool waves, when from her sweet
Bosom his burning thirst is quench'd;
   Then mark how, with disdainful feet,
He kicks her banks, and from the place
That thus refresh'd him, moves with sullen pace.

Thus shalt thou be despis'd, fair maid,
   When by thy sated lover tasted;
What first he did with tears invade,
   Shall afterwards in scorn be wasted;
When all thy virgin springs grow dry,
And no springs left, but in thine eye.

The three foregoing Pieces are by Thomas Carew, whose admirers were the first men of the age in which he lived. Lord
Clarendon says, " Carew was a person of a pleasant and facetious

wit, whose poems, for the sharpness of the fancy, and elegance of
the language in which that fancy was spread, were at least equal,
if not superior, to any of that time."   Born, 1580; died, 1639.
His poems were published in 1772, by Davis.

FLY THE FAIR SEX.

YE happy swains, whose hearts are free
   From love's imperial chain,
Take warning, and be taught by me
   To avoid the enchanting pain;
Fatal the wolves to trembling flocks,
   Fierce winds to blossoms prove,
To careless seamen, hidden rocks,
   To human quiet, love.

Fly the fair sex, if bliss you prize,
   The snake's beneath the flower;
Who ever gaz'd on beauteous eyes,
   That tasted quiet more?
How faithless is the lover's joys!
   How constant is their care!
The kind, with falsehood do destroy,
   The cruel, with despair.

By SIR GEORGE ETHEREGE; this celebrated wit was born near
London, 1634; author of three plays, and a volume of sprightly
poetry.   His accomplishments procured him the favour of James
the Second's Queen, to whom he had dedicated his " Man of Mode."
.Report says that he came to an untimely end, by an accident which
befel him at Ratisbon.

TO CHLOE.

CHLOE! why wish you that your years
  Would backward run, till they meet mine,
That perfect likeness, which endears
  Things unto things, might us combine?
Our ages so in date agree,
That twins do differ more than we.

There are two births: the one, when light
  First strikes the new awaken'd sense;
The other, when two souls unite,
  And we must count our life from thence;
When you lov'd me, and I lov'd you,
Then both of us were born a-new.

Love then to us did new souls give,
  And in these souls did plant new powers;
Since when another life we live,
  The breath we breathe, is his, not ours;
Love makes those young, whom age doth chill,
And whom he finds young, keeps young still.

Love like that angel that shall call
  Our bodies from the silent grave;
Unto one age doth raise us all,
  None too much, none too little have.
Nay, that the difference may be none,
He makes two not alike, but one.

And now since you and I are such,
    Tell me what's your's, and what is mine?
Our eyes, our ears, our taste, smell, touch,
    Do like our souls in one combine:
So by this, I as well may be
    To old for you, as you for me.

From Poems and Songs, by WILLIAM CARTWRIGHT, born 1611, died 1643. His poetry, says Campbell, in his specimens of the British Poets, may be ranked as the violet, humble but sweet of smell. Ben Johnson says of him, "My son Cartwright writes all like a man." He was of Christ's College, Oxford. Became Proctor of the University, and Lecturer on metaphysics. He was cut off by fever, aged 32, and had the honour to be regarded by his sovereign and queen, who were in Oxford at the time of his death.

GO LOVELY ROSE.

Go lovely rose!
Tell her that wastes her time, and me,
    That now she knows,
When I resemble her to thee,
How sweet and fair she seems to be.

Tell her that's young,
And shuns to have her graces spied,
    That hadst thou sprung
In deserts, where no men abide,
Thou must have uncommended died.

Small is the worth
Of beauty from the light retir'd;
Bid her come forth,
Suffer herself to be desir'd,
And not blush so to be admir'd.

Then die! that she
The common fate of all things rare
May read in thee:
How small a part of time they share,
That are so wondrous sweet and fair.

The author of this beautiful lyric was EDMUND WALLER, born 1605, died 1687. His poetical pieces are easy, smooth, and generally elegant; even the gruff and irascible Ritson esteems him the best song writer, as well as the best poet, of Charles I.'s time.

IN COMMENDATION OF MUSIC.

WHEN whispering strains do softly steal
  With creeping passion through the heart;
And when at every touch we feel
  Our pulses beat, and bear a part:
When threats can make a heart-string quake,
  Philosophy can scarce deny,
  The soul consists of harmony.

When unto heavenly joys we feign,
  Whate'er the soul affecteth most;
Which only thus—we can explain
  By music of the winged host,

Whose lays we think, make stars to wink:
   Philosophy can scarce deny,
   The soul consists of harmony.

O lull me, lull me, charming air,
   My senses rock with wonder sweet!
Like snow on wool, thy fallings are
   Soft, like a spirit are thy feet;
Grief, who need fear, that hath an ear?
   Down let him lie, and slumbering die,
   And change his soul for harmony.

The above Sonnet is the composition of WILLIAM STRODE, or STROUDE, taken from a small miscellany, called " Wit restored," 1658, 12mo. He was born, says Ellis, about 1600. Became D. D. and Canon of Christ Church, having served the office of Proctor and public Orator to the University; and had the reputation of being a good preacher, and exquisite speaker, and an eminent poet.

THE DEW NO MORE SHALL WEEP.

THE dew no more shall weep,
   The primrose's pale cheek to deck;
The dew no more shall sleep,
   Nuzzled in the lily's neck:
Much rather would it tremble here,
And leave them both to be thy tear.

Not the soft gold which
   Steals from the amber weeping tree,
Makes sorrow half so rich,
   As the drops distill'd from thee:
Sorrow's best jewels be in these
Caskets, of which Heaven keeps the keys.

When sorrow would be seen
   In her bright majesty,
For she is a Queen!
   Then is she dress'd by none but thee,
Then, and only then, she wears
Her richest pearls;—I mean thy tears.

Not in the evening's eye
   When they red with weeping are;
For the sun that dies,
   Sits sorrow with a face so fair:
No where but here doth meet,
Sweetness so sad, sadness so sweet.

The above Song is by the REV. RICHARD CRAWSHAW, who died about 1650. His poetry, says Campbell, is full of tenderness and beauty, sentiment and imagery. His versification is melodious. Expressions delicate and luxurious. Works numerous, and chiefly upon religious subjects.

TO LUCASTA.

TELL me not, sweet, I am unkind,
   That from the nunnery
Of thy chaste breast, and quiet mind,
   To war and arms I fly.

True, a new mistress now I chase,
  The first foe in the field;
And with a stronger faith embrace,
  A sword, a horse, a shield.

Yet this inconstancy is such,
  As you too shall adore;
I could not love thee, dear, so much,
  Loved I not honour more.

ELINDA'S GLOVE.

THOU snowy farm, with thy five tenements,
  Tell thy white mistress here was one
That call'd to pay his daily rents;
  But she a-gathering flowers and hearts is gone,
  And thou left void to rude possession.

But grieve not pretty ermine cabinet,
  Thy alabaster lady will come home:
If not, what tenant can they fit
  The slender turnings of thy narrow room,
  But must ejected be, by his own doom.

Then give me leave, to leave my rent with thee,
  Five kisses, one unto each place;
For though the lute's too high for me,
  Yet servants knowing minikin nor base,
  Are still allow'd to fiddle with the case.

TO THE ROSE.

SWEET serene sky-like flower,
Haste to adorn her bower;
    From thy long cloudy bed,
    Shoot forth thy damask head.

Vermilion ball that's given
From lip to lip in heaven;
    Love's couches' coverlid,
    Haste, haste, to make her bed.

See! rosy is her bower,
Her floor is all this flower;
    Her bed a rosy nest,
    By a bed of roses press'd.

The three foregoing Songs are by Colonel RICHARD LOVELACE, born 1618. Exquisitely beautiful in his person, with a mind elegantly and classically endowed, he was one of the gayest and sprightliest courtiers of Charles I.'s reign. His own calamities followed those of the party to which he belonged—imprisoned and blighted in all his fortunes, brought on a state of despairing wretchedness, which ended in a fatal consumption, and terminated his life in a garret, 1658.

Colonel Lovelace's unfortunate demise is doubted, as given by Anthony Wood in the second volume of his Athenæ; and some say that his estates were not forfeited, but descended to the family; yet Edward Wyld confirms Wood's assertions, and writes that he died poor, and in a cellar.

His poems are chaste, classical, imaginative, and beautiful: they were published in 8vo. in 1649, and again in 1659.

THE HUNT IS UP.

DARE ye hunt our hallow'd green?
None but fairies here are seen:
Down and sleep, wail and weep,
Pinch him black, and pinch him blue,
That seeks to steal a lover true.
When ye come to hear us sing,
Or to tread our fairy ring,
Pinch him black, and pinch him blue,
Thus our nails shall handle you.

A wild hunting chorus, meant to represent the starting of a chase, is attached to the above; nearly unintelligible however, unless accompanied by its music, which has been arranged for four voices by Byrd, and entered by him into Queen Elizabeth's Virginal, and also into the Lady Nevil's Music-book, who appears to have been Byrd's pupil. This curious relict, with accompaniments, apparently adapted for the horn, is engrossed into our old M. S. collection of airs, alluded to in page 48. This M. S. volume, we may mention, in passing, contains 158 song tunes in parts, independent of sacred music; while the airs of several songs contained in this section, are to be found here, pricked down with great care, in the square or lozenge note, having the first line of each chant generally appended to its corresponding music. No date is attached to the M. S. but the latest tune in the volume is above two hundred years old.

DIRGE.

I'LL go to my love, where he lies in the deep,
And in my embraces my dearest shall sleep:

When we wake, the kind dolphins together shall throng,
And in chariots of shells shall draw us along:
 Ah! ah! my love's dead! there was not a bell,
  But a Triton's shell,
 To ring, to ring, out his knell.

The orient pearl which the ocean bestows,
With coral we'll mix, and a crown so compose;
The sea-nymphs shall sigh, and envy our bliss,
We will teach them to laugh, and their cockles to kiss:
 Ah! ah! my love's dead!

For my love sleeps now in a watery grave,
He hath nothing to show for his tomb but a wave;
I'll kiss his cold lips, not the coral more red,
That grows where he lies in his watery bed:
 Ah! ah! my love's dead!

From Tixhall Poetry, published 1813, by EDWARD CLIFFORD, Esq. For a curious and interesting account of these ancient M. SS. see Drake's " Evenings in Autumn."

THE ROYAL NUN.

CANST thou, Marina, leave the world,
 The world that is devotion's bane,
Where crowns are toss'd, and sceptres hurl'd,
 Where lust and proud ambition reign?
Canst thou thy costly robes forbear,
 To live with us in poor attire;
Canst thou from courts to cells repair,
 To sing at midnight in the quire?

Canst thou forget the golden bed,
    Where thou might'st sleep beyond the morn,
On mats to lay thy royal head,
    And have thy beauteous tresses shorn?
Canst thou resolve to fast all day,
    And weep and groan to be forgiven;
Canst thou in broken slumbers pray,
    And by afflictions merit heaven?

Say Voterisse, can this be done?
    Whilst we the grace divine implore;
The world shall lose the battles won,
    And sin shall never chain thee more.
The gate to bliss doth open stand,
    And all my penance is in view;
The world, upon the other hand,
    Cries out, " O do not bid adieu!"

What, what can pomp and glory do;
    Or what can human powers persuade;
That mind that hath a heaven in view,
    How can it be by earth betray'd?
Haste then, oh! haste, to take me in,
    For ever lock Religion's door;
Secure me from the charms of sin,
    And let me see the world no more.

This beautiful poem of the Royal Nun, says Dr. Drake, is from a M.S. dated 1662; but in all probability it is several years older. Who was its author, is not known. It evidently bears a strong resemblance to Dr. Percy's popular song, " O Nannie wilt thou gang wi' me."

THE five following Songs have been excerpted from a scarce and rather curious work, commonly known by the name of the Aberdeen Cantus, entitled, " Songs and Fancies to three, four, or five parts, both apt for voices or viols; with a brief Introduction to Music, as taught by Thomas Davidson in the Music-School of Aberdeen. By John Forbes."

The Cantus contains in all, sixty-seven Songs, including translations from the Italian at the end of the volume; the greater part of these, however, will be found more curious than interesting to song-collectors of the present day, their tenor for the most part being either of a quaint love, or religious cast, accordant with the taste of the times in which they had been gleaned for the Cantus, by Forbes and Davidson.

It also is provoking to find such a paucity of Scottish songs, or Scottish airs, within the pages of this, the first printed musical work in our own country; and that at a time, too, when several of those pieces whose loss we now grieve for, must have been in circulation around the very localities wherein the materials for the above Cantus were collected.

Pinkerton, in his " Scottish Poems," prelim. xxxiv. says the Cantus is a work he wishes much to see; he likewise states the impression of 1682, as being the third edition. Allowing then, the impression of 1666 to have been the second, when did the first appear, as John Forbes is stated, in the history of early Scottish printers, to have commenced business about 1660? We understand the curious "Pleugh Song," "My hearty service to you, my Lord," &c. is only found in the second edition, while the first and third want it.

COME, SWEET LOVE.

COME, sweet love, let sorrow cease,
   Banish frowns, leave off dissension;
Love's war makes the sweetest peace,
   Hearts uniting by contention;
Sunshine follows after rain,
    Sorrows ceasing, this is pleasing,
     All proves fair again;
    After sorrow cometh joy:
Trust me, prove me, try me, love me,
    This will cure annoy.

Winter hides his frosty face,
   Blushing ever to be moved;
Spring returns with pleasing grace,
   Flora's treasures are renewed;
Lambs rejoice to see the spring,
    Leaping, skipping, sporting, tripping;
     Birds for joy do sing:
    Let your springs of joy renew,
Colling, clapping, kissing, blessing,
    And give love his due.

See this sunshine of thine eyes,
   Clouded now with dark disdaining;
Shall such stormy tempests rise
   To set love's fair day a-raining!
Men are glad, the sky being clear,
   Lightly toying, sporting, joying,
     With their lovely peer;
   But are sad to see the shower,
Sadly dropping, louring, pouring,
     Turning sweet to sour.

Then, sweet love, disperse this cloud,
   Which procures this woful toying;
When each warbler sings aloud,
   Killing hearts with overjoying;
Every dove doth seek her mate,
   Jointly billing, she is willing,
     Sweets of love to take:
   With such wars let us contend,
Wooing, doing, wedding, bedding,
     This our strife shall end.

LOVE WILL FIND OUT THE WAY.

Over the mountains
   And over the waves,
Over the fountains
   And under the graves;
Over the floods that are deepest,
   Which do Neptune obey;
Over rocks that are steepest,
   Love will find out the way.

Where there is no place
  For the glow-worm to lie;
Where there is no space
  For the receipt of a fly;
Where the midge dare not venture,
  Lest herself fast she lay;
If love come, he will enter,
  And soon find out his way.

You may esteem him
  A child in his force,
Or you may deem him
  A coward, which is worse;
But if she, whom love doth honour,
  Be conceal'd from the day,
Set a thousand guards upon her,
  Love will find out the way.

Some think to lose him,
  Which is too unkind;
And some do suppose him,
  Poor thing, to be blind:
But if ne'er so close ye wall him,
  Do the best that ye may,
Blind love, if so ye call him,
  He will find out the way.

You may train the eagle
  To stoop to your fist;
Or you may inveigle
  The phœnix of the east;

The lioness, ye may move her
 To give o'er her prey,
But you'll ne'er stop a lover,
 He will find out his way.

THE FORCE OF LOVE.

The lowest trees have tops, the ant her gall,
 The fly her spleen, the little spark its heat;
The slender hairs cast shadows though but small,
 And bees have stings although they be not great;
Seas have their source, and so have little springs,
And love is love in beggars as in kings.

Where waters smoothest run, deep are the fords;
 The dial slurs, yet none perceives it move;
The firmest faith is in the fewest words;
 The turtles cannot sing, and yet they love.
True hearts have eyes, and ears, no tongues to speak,
They hear and see, and sigh, and then they break.

WOE WORTH THE TIME.

Woe worth the time, and eke the place,
 That she was to me known;
For since I first beheld her face,
 My heart was never mine own, my Jo,
 My heart was never mine own.

Sometime I lived at liberty,
　But now, I do not so;
She hath my heart so faithfully,
　That I can love no mo, my Jo,
　That I can love no mo.

To be refus'd of love, alas!
　All earthly things adieu;
My mistress she is merciless,
　And will not on me rue,[1] my Jo,
　And will not on me rue.

Now am I left all comfortless,
　And no remead can crave;
My pains they are remeadyless,
　And all the wyte you have, my Jo,
　And all the wyte you have.

O LUSTY MAY.

O lusty May, with Flora queen,
The balmy drops from Phœbus' sheen,
　Prelucent beam before the day,
By thee Diana groweth green,
　Through gladness of this lusty May.

Then Esperus that is so bright,
To woful hearts, she casts her light,
　O'er buds that bloom on every brae;
And showers are shed forth of that sight,
　Through gladness of this lusty May.

1 Rue, Have pity.

Birds on boughs, of every birth,
Rejoicing notes, making their mirth,
   Right pleasantly upon the spray;
With flourishings o'er field and firth,
   Through gladness of this lusty May.

All lovers that are in care,
To their ladies then do repair,
   In fresh mornings before the day;
And are in mirth aye mair and mair,
   Through gladness of this lusty May.

Of every month in the year,
To mirthful May there is no peer,
   Her glistering garments are so gay;
You lovers all make merry cheer,
   Through gladness of this lusty May.

The above relict is of considerable antiquity, mention being made of it in the " Complaint of Scotland," 1549. Four stanzas of " Lusty May," are copied into the Bannatyne M.SS. while a complete copy will be found in the " Aberdeen Cantus." A faithful reprint of this Song, from the Bannatyne M.SS. has lately been given to the public, along with its original music, by Mr. David Laing, in his Notes (p. 99) to Alexander Scott's Poems.

THE OLD MAN'S WISH.

IF I live to grow old, as I find I go down,
Let this be my fate: in a fair country town,
Let me have a warm house, with a stone at my gate,
And a cleanly young girl to rub my bald pate.

May I govern my passions with an absolute sway;
And grow wiser and better as my strength wears away,
Without gout or stone, by a gentle decay.

In a country town, by a murmuring brook,
With the ocean at distance on which I may look;
With a green spacious plain, without hedge or stile,
And an easy pad nag to ride out a mile.
  May I govern my passions, &c.

With Horace and Petrarch, and one or two more
Of the best wits that liv'd in the ages before;
With a dish of roast mutton, not venison nor teal,
And clean, though coarse, linen at every meal.
  May I govern my passions, &c.

With a pudding on Sundays, and stout humming liquor,
And remnants of Latin to puzzle the vicar;
With a hidden reserve of good Burgundy wine,
To drink the king's health as oft as we dine.
  May I govern my passions, &c.

With a courage undaunted may I face my last day!
And, when I am dead, may the better sort say,
In the morning when sober, in the evening when mellow,
He is gone, and has left not behind him his fellow!
  For he govern'd his passions with an absolute sway;
  And grew wiser and better as his strength wore away,
  Without gout or stone, by a gentle decay.

This beautiful contemplative Song is by DR. WALTER POPE,
half-brother to Bishop Wilkins, published by him in 1693, six
years after he had resigned his professorship of astronomy in

Gresham College. He was author of several humorous ballads, and of many serious treatises in prose, which are enumerated in Dr. Ward's Lives of the Gresham Professors.

QUEEN MARY'S FAREWELL TO FRANCE.

AH! pleasant land of France, farewell;
That country dear, where many a year
Of infant youth I lov'd to dwell;
Farewell for ever happy days!
The ship which parts our loves, conveys
But half of me:—one-half behind
I leave with thee, dear France, to prove
A token of our endless love,
And bring the other to thy mind.

This delicate little sonnet is given by RITSON, from the original French of the thrice unfortunate and accomplished Mary Queen of Scots, apparently written by her upon leaving France, after the death of her first husband Francis II. Mary's early troubles are aptly delineated by Hogg, in the following couplets:

In one short year, her hopes all cross'd,
A parent, husband, kingdom lost!
And all ere eighteen summers shed
Their honours o'er her royal head.

TELL HER I LOVE.

ONLY tell her that I love,
Leave the rest to her and fate;
Some kind planet from above,
May perhaps her pity move:

Lovers on their stars must wait,
　　Only tell her that I love.

Why, oh why, should I despair?
　　Mercy's pictur'd in her eye;
If she once vouchsafe to hear,
　　Welcome hope, and welcome fear:
She's too good to let me die,
　　Why, oh why, should I despair?

The above is by LORD CUTTS, a soldier of most hardy bravery in King William's wars.   In 1701, he was colonel of the Coldstream Guards, when Steel was indebted to him for his military commission, and in gratitude inscribed to him his first work, " The Christian Hero."   On the accession of Queen Anne, he was made lieutenant-general of the forces in Holland; commander-in-chief of the forces in Ireland, under the Duke of Ormond, in 1704, and afterwards one of the Lord Justices of that kingdom, to keep him out of the way of action, a circumstance which broke his heart.   He died at Dublin, about the year 1706.   Several copies of verses, and eleven songs, are all his published remains.

In page 29, part of a sentence in note to " Whence comes my love," has unfortunately been omitted, which ought to have stood thus:—From a M.S. of JOHN HARRINGTON's, dated 1564, and inserted into the Nugæ Antiquæ, a Miscellaneous Collection of original papers in prose and verse, written in the reigns of Henry VIII. Edward VI. Mary, Elizabeth, James I. &c. by Sir John Harrington, the translator of Ariosto, and others who lived in these times, 12mo. Robinson and Roberts, 1767.   This John Harrington, &c. (as is continued in note).

SECTION II.

MISCELLANEOUS POEMS,

BY

SIR WILLIAM MURE, KNIGHT,

OF ROWALLAN,

AUTHOR OF "THE TRVE CRVCIFIXE."

WITH BIOGRAPHICAL & RELATIVE NOTICES.

By John Fullarton, Esq.

NOTICES OF SIR WILLIAM MURE.

It would seem confessed, in assailing the " ancient Faith," little proved more formidable than those satires and pasquils, for which, in particular, Sir David Lindsay stands so pre-eminently distinguished. Modified to the progress of events, writings of this nature continued to appear, no doubt with decreasing interest and point, down at least to the final period of the Revolution.

Considerably previous to the renewed outbreakings in the time of Charles the First, Sir William Mure of Rowallan published an elaborate and lengthy poem, under the title of the *Trve Crvcifixe*, and by which, in this class of literature, his name has not yet utterly been forgotten. Haply, therefore, at least to those solicitous of such matters, a selection of the lighter emanations of the muse of the *Trve Crvcifixe*, may not be deemed wholly uninteresting. Nor, peradventure, may the few casual memorials subjoined of its zealous author, at this distance of time, be viewed as greatly less acceptable; and it is only regretted, that neither the nature of the present compilation, nor the means of obtaining materials, enable doing more suitable justice to the subject.

The family of Rowallan in Ayrshire, is amongst the most ancient and honourably connected of the baronial rank in the country. Elizabeth Mure, wife of the Second Robert of Scotland—from whom have descended the succeeding Royal line of Stuart, and their illustrious successors to the present time—was a daughter of the house of Rowallan.[1]

SIR WILLIAM MURE, a selection of whose poesies here follow, was the lineal descendant and successor of the family. About the year 1593, his father, Sir William Mure of Rowallan, married, first, when very young, Elizabeth, daughter of Montgomery of Hazelhead, and by whom our author was the eldest of two sons, and a daughter married to Boyd of Pinkill. This lady appears to have been daughter to Hugh Montgomery of Hazelhead, Ayrshire (descended of Eglintoun), by Marion Sempill,[2] daughter of Lord Sempill, and sister to MONTGOMERY, author of the *Cherrie and the Slae.* In a metrical address, now first printed, to Charles, Prince of Wales, afterwards Charles the First, Sir William Mure thus alludes to his near connection with the Poet:

My Muse, quhich noght doth challenge worthy fame,
Save from MONTGOMERY sche her birth doth clayme.

[1] An interesting genealogical memoir of the family, written by our author, was lately published, from the original MS. at Glasgow, by the Rev. William Muir. In which the curious reader may find an account of the ancestry of Rowallan detailed at length.

[2] Crawford, followed by subsequent genealogists, calls her *Janet;* but in an original writ belonging to the family of Blair, Ayrshire, wherein "Hew Montgomerie of Heiselheid" grants a reversion of lands to John Blair of that ilk, 1581, she is named Marion, and was then living.

There certainly still remain indubitable indications of Sir William Mure's early proficiency as a scholar; and, as we learn from himself, before attaining his twentieth year, he composed an English metrical version of Virgil's *Dido and Æneas*—some further notice of which afterwards:

> But pardon, Maro, if myn infant Muse
> (To *twyse two lustres* scarce of yeirs attained).

Yet, in his education, it appears not that he was ever destined otherwise than merely to support, in his succession, the hereditary rank and condition of the family, in the several relations of society and the state: indeed, in the extremely limited field of that period, professional pursuits of any kind seem to have been but little thought of by the eldest branches of the more wealthy families. Before this time, Kilmarnock, in the near vicinity of the family residence, had risen to the rank of a burgh, and so, probably, might afford him the means of rudimental instruction. And there is perhaps still more probability, that he completed his education at the then newly revived University of Glasgow, under the direction of the eminent Principal Boyd, for whom it is apparent he always entertained the highest veneration: it is at least so far presumable, his brother Hugb, afterwards a clergyman in England, in 1618, was matriculated in that College.

Before fully completing his majority, in 1615, he married Anna, daughter of Dundas of Newliston;[1] and by whom he had five sons and six daughters: of the latter, the only one mentioned to have been married, was Elizabeth, wife of Uchter Knox of Ranfurlie—for what seems known, the last of that race directly descending, from which the reformer has ordinarily been deduced. The eldest son, William, the friend of Guthrie of Fenwick,[2] succeeded his father, as Mure of Rowallan; Alexander was killed in the Irish rebellion, 1641; Robert, a major in the army, married the "Lady Newhall" in Fife; John was designed of Fenwickhill; and Patrick, probably the youngest, was created a baronet of Nova-Scotia, in 1662. He married, secondly, dame Jane Hamilton, Lady Duntreath; and of this marriage there were two sons and two daughters—James, Hugh, Jane, and Marion.

Following the course of the present inquiry, over no inconsiderable space of comparative public tranquillity in the history of those excited times, little occurs to disquiet the peaceful tenor of our author's domestic felicity—the elements of which, under more favourable circumstances, perhaps but few ever possessed in a higher degree. A taste for building and rural embellishment, seems discoverable in the family of Rowallan at a period when decorations of this nature were confessedly but little regarded in

1 John, first Earl of Stair, born about 1648, married Elizabeth, daughter and heiress of Sir John Dundas of Newliston, in the county of Linlithgow, Knight. This lady was mother of the second Earl, so well known in his military capacity.—*Peer. voce* Stair.

2 See Letters of the Rev. William Guthrie to Sir William Mure, younger of Rowallan, &c. just published by Mr. Oliphant, Edinburgh.

Scotland: and in these refinements, Sir William certainly fell nothing behind, if he did not rather surpass the slowly advancing spirit of his time; besides planting and other ameliorations, he made various additions to the family mansion, and "reformed the whole house exceedingly."

At last, however, the internal struggles betwixt the unbending assertors of presbytery, and the no less frantic policy of the court, to retain at least some modification of the former ceremonial, came to a crisis in the noted assembly at Glasgow, 1638. As a last alternative, the covenanters found themselves committed to the taking up of arms. Consequently, early in summer 1639, on the Royal preparations at York, the army of the covenant began to assemble, and about the beginning of June, formed the celebrated camp on Dunse-Law. Ayrshire, " according to the common undervaluing which was in the country, sent out 1200 foot and horsemen, under Lord Loudon's conduct as crowner, and Mr. David Dickson [of Irvine] as minister."[1] The presence of the Earl of Eglintoun, an energetic and spirited nobleman, in consequence of a threatened descent from Ireland, appears to have been required for a time in the western parts; but Lord Montgomery, his son, attended the march, and the Earl afterwards, " though late," joined the camp of the famed Leslie.

Of this subsidy of the county, Sir William Mure of Rowallan had the command of a company of his own

---

[1] *Baillie*, I. 164, who remarks: " Our soldiers were all lusty and full of courage; the most of them stout young plowmen; great cheerfulness in the face of all."

neighbourhood and tenants: how conscientiously all were animated with the purest feelings of good-will to both prince and people, happily time has long so clearly developed, as entirely to supersede all future comment. The following short letter of Lord Eglintoun on this occasion, however, whilst creditable to our author, may perhaps be deemed otherwise curious.

" *To my Richt wourschipfoull and most louing frind, Sir Wll. Mour of Rouallan, knicht, younger.*

" Richt wourschipfoull and most louing freind—I long to heir from you, therfoir I will intret you to let me heir from you with all occasiounis; for I expek my best intelligence from you; for quhat ever passes let me knau, and pray you have a cair of your sogeris, be I pleding for them, for it will gar yourself be moir respekit. I pray God to derck you all, and so preserve you from all danger. I rest,

Your most louing freind to serue you,

Eglintoun the 20. of   EGLINTOUN.
May, 1639.

[*P. S.*] Ze sall resaue a nanser of the Gentlemen['s] letter heirin inclosit—I expek thair ansour."

The result of this step is well known. Whether Rowallan personally engaged in any of the intermediate proceedings of those lamentable times, appears not. He was a member of the Scots Parliament, for Ayrshire, 1643. In the beginning of 1644, he accompanied the Scots army in their last expedition into England; and after a variety of services, part of which he narrates in a letter to his son,

March 12, he was present, and wounded, in the memorable conflict of Marston-moor, July 2. Again, in August following, he was engaged at the storming of Newcastle, where, for some time, the command of the regiment devolved upon him; Colonel Hobert and some other of the officers being absent of wounds received at the late battle. This was probably our author's ultimate campaign; although the events which immediately followed, in rapid succession, would have afforded an ample and pregnant field for the mere soldier " to bustle in." But for more than the last ten years of his life, we have not been fortunate enough to meet with any material notice of him. He died some time in the year 1657.

Though no very high rank can certainly be assigned Sir William Mure as a poet, yet it is sufficiently evident, by his performances that way, he enjoyed no inconsiderable reputation in his own day; nor at the present time, when the few unperished blossoms of a vigorous and less adulterated age are being more justly appreciated, would any considerable portion of his writings at all seem wholly unworthy of preservation: whilst, for a peculiar purity of thought and smoothness of diction, without any thing ininvidious, many of Rowallan's compilations may stand a comparison with others, the productions of far more pretending names, and than mere rarity, may justly lay claim to preservation on a far different and surer foundation.

The earliest of his printed labours occurs in the *Muses Welcome*, 1618, a collection of poetical panegyrics on the visit of King James to Scotland the preceding year—Sir

William's is addressed to the King, at Hamilton. In 1628, he published a translation of Trochrig's beautiful Latin poem—*Hecatombe Christiana*,—" Invected in English Sapphicks, from the Latine of that Reverend, Religious, and Learned Divine, Mr. Robert Boyd of Trochorege." Copies of both these rare compilations, it is believed, are preserved in the library of the Faculty of Advocates.

But the most considerable, best known, and latest of Rowallan's published poesies, remains in the *Trve Crvcifixe for Trve Catholickes*—Edin. 1629, 12mo. This is a work now of considerable curiosity, as relating to a subject and period not only instructive but deeply interesting; though as a mere literary composition, doubtless out of sight the most arid of any thing of the author's preserved: and in truth, is at most little other than a mere versified and laborious *exposé* of that prime symbol of Romish "idolatry," the obnoxious Crucifix. He has not, however, in the attack, always foregone the weapons of humour and ridicule; and it must be confessed, passages of considerable ingenuity and caustic point more frequently occur, than a hasty glance at the volume will generally seem to suggest. The following brief but comprehensive picture of ancient priestcraft, furnishes a pretty equal specimen of what is meant:

> Thus do those *Glow-wormes*, which but shine by night,
> The substance of the world suck vp by slight;
> By shows of holynesse, by secret stealth,
> Congesting mountaines of entysing wealth,
> To which, as *Ravens* which doe a Carion see,
> Trowps of *Church-orders*, swarms of *Shavelings* flie;

Of which none idle, all on work are set:
By cous'ning miracles, some doe credite get;
To cristen bels, tosse beads, they some appoint;
Some crosse, some creepe, some sprinkle, some anoynt;
Some hallow candles, palmes, crisme, ashes, wax;
Some penitents admitt to kisse the Pax!

And of a different order, the following, at the opening
of the poem, seems strikingly expressed:

But muse I could not, how from time to time,
Man—but a masse of animated slime;
A cloud of dust, tos'd by vncertaine breath;
A wormeling weake, soone to stoupe downe to death!

It has been observed, this was the latest of our author's
publications: his writings which remain in MS. seem
fully as considerable, and certainly not inferior in merit.
The most important of these are, an entire version of the
Psalms, and a metrical translation of Virgil's *Dido and
Æneas*. The latter, as formerly alluded to, he essayed
at an unusually early time of life for such an undertaking.
The following are his opening stanzas of this celebrated
poem:

I sing Æneas' fortunes, while on fyr,
    Of dying Troy he takes his last farewell;
Queen Dido's love, and cruell Juno's ire,
    With equal fervor which he both doth [did] feel.
Path'd wayes I trace, as Theseus in his neid,
Conducted by a loyall virgin's threid.

But pardon, Maro, if myn infant muse
    (To twyse two lustres scarce of yeirs attained),
Such task to treat (vnwisely bold) doth choose,
    As thy sweet voyce hath earst divinely strained!

L

And in grave numbers of bewitching verse,
Ravisht with wonder all the vniverse.

But, ravisht with a vehement 'desyre,
   Those paths to trace, which yeilds ane endles name!
By thee to climb Parnassus I aspyre,
   And by thy feathers to impen my fame,
Nothing asham'd, thir colours to display,
Vnder thy conduct, as my first assay.

Sacred Apollo! lend thy Cynthia light,
   Which, by thy gloriows rayes, reflexe doth shyne,
That I, partaking of thy purest spright,
   May grave, anew, on tyme's immortall shryne,
In homely stile, those sweit delicious ayers,
In which thy muse so admirable appears.

And ye, Pierian maids, ye sacred nyne!
   Which haunt Parnassus and the Pegas spring,
Infuse your furie in my weak ingyne,
   That (mask'd with Maro) sweetly I may sing;
And warble foorth this hero's changing state,
Eliza's love, and last her tragick fate.

Now bloody warre (the mistres of debait,
   Attendit still with discorde, death, dispair;
The child of wrath, nurst by despightfull hait,
   With visage pale, stern lookes, and snaiky hair),
By Grecian armes, old Troy had beatne downe,
And rais'd the ten-yeirs siege from Priam's towne:

Whose brasen teeth her walls did shake asunder,
   And staitly turrets levell'd with the ground:
Insulting Greeks, with fyre and sword did thunder;
   And both alike the sone and syre confound,
The maid and matron: striving to compence
Fair Helen's rapt, and Paris' proud offence.

The same measure is continued throughout the whole three books into which this poem, consisting of 407 stanzas, is divided.—This principal effort of the author's, the MS. of which is in the most beautiful preservation, and probably is unique, would form an advantageous separate publication; and, should encouragement offer, may yet be attempted.

The Psalms, of which several copies exist, appear to have been completed in the year 1639; about which time, the subject of an improved Psalmody seems to have occupied very general attention. Many superior passages of sacred poetry occur in this attempt of Sir William's; and it is said, the Committee of the General Assembly appointed to revise Mr. Rous', the version finally adopted, were instructed nevertheless to avail themselves of the "help of Rowallan's." Mr. Muir has given some specimens of our author's Psalter, in the appendix to the family history, before alluded to.

From the poetical remains of Sir William Mure, we have selected the following varieties. They are all transcribed with the utmost fidelity and care, from his own original manuscripts, the orthography of part only, being altered to modern rule, whilst any thing emendatory attempted, is always separately noted. The following rubric appears in the author's own hand :

" Amorouse Essayes, passionatly exprest, contryved in a Poetical Rapsodie, Sigh'd forth by Ane Lower. In Elegies, Sonets, Songs, The comitragical history of Dido and Æneas, tracing ye steps of ye best of Latin Poets, wt. wthers smal works, being all ye Infant Labours and very furstlings of ye Authors Muse. By Sr. W. Muire, Yo. of Rowalen."

BEAUTY'S TRIUMPH.

WHILE Beauty by a pleasant spring reposes,
  With fairest ranks of trees o'ershadow'd under,
The cooling air with calmest blasts rejoices,
  To sport her with her locks, o'ercome with wonder;
So then, admiring her most heavenly feature,
I marvell'd much if she was form'd by nature.

The smiling blinks sent from her wanton eyes,
  Had force to rob proud Cupid of his darts;
Her shamefaced blushing smiles who ever sees,
  Must part perforce, leaving behind their hearts:
I stood astonish'd, greedy to behold,
So rare perfection as cannot be told.

She then perceiving me in thought perplex'd,
  With voice angelical did thus begin:
"Thy gesture doth bewray thy mind is vex'd,
  With crosses compass'd, and environ'd in:
Show, then, if love, or what misfortune else,
Such signs of sorrow in thy soul compels."

"No cross at all, fair dame; no force in love
  Can ought disquiet or perturb my mind;
The wonders now are present me doth move—
  To see heaven's excellence in human kind."
"No! Cupid thee molests, cease to deny him."
"Fie! treacherous love, fond Cupid I defy him."

Even at this time the blinded god arriv'd,
   His bow bent in his hand ready to knock;
But while he aim'd, of power quite depriv'd,
   Himself he bound in his own flattering yoke:
Feeding his eyes on beauty's tempting looks,
His pain he thought to ease with baited hooks.

So boil'd with flames, vex'd both with fear and tears,
   Out of the anguish of his heart did 'plain:
" Ah! matchless dame, whom all the world admires,
   Pity, I pray, my never ceasing pain;
Do not thy rigour unto me extend,
Whom once no mortal durst presume t' offend.

" But now at last o'ercome, I humbly yield,
   Save then, or slay a captive begging grace;
Receive in sign that thou hast won the field,
   The bow, the shafts, the quiver, and the brace;
'Once which I brook'd, but now without envy,
 I yield to thee, more worthy them than I."

The homage ended, and the goddess arm'd,
   With proud, presuming Cupid's conquer'd spoil;
He then remitted, fled away unharm'd,
   But, woes me! left behind his torturing toil.
She spying me, yet unacquaint in love,
Her new got darts, through my poor heart did rove.

" Sport now," she says, "with Cupid! boldly try him;
   In love, if any force, now prove, I pray;—
Too late, I fear, thou rue thou did espy him,
   Thine insolence 'gainst him or he repay."

Disdainfully delivering thus her words,
No small displeasure to my soul affords.

I yet a novice in my new learn'd art,
   Admir'd so quick a change from joy to woe;
Doubted myself even if it was my heart,
   My tears which trickling from mine eyes did go;
But, ah! in vain, for yet my wound did bleed;
No spates of tears could quench the boiling lead.

I flamed, I froze, in love, in cold disdain;
   Died in despair, in hope again I lived:
All pleasures past aggrieved my present pain,
   Her frown did kill, her smile again revived.
While death I wish'd, life then refused to leave me;
Live while I would, death they propon'd to reave me.

While in this weak estate, all means I sought
   To be avenged on him, whose shafts did grieve me;
Alas! a faint pursuit—I further'd nought,
   For he, now Cupid, now a sprite, did leave me;—
Thus metamorphos'd, fled away for aid
In beauty's lips, where I durst naught invade.

Then favour begg'd; pity moved her consent,—
   Render the fortress and his surest shield;
Great search I made to make the wretch repent
   His bold attempts, entreating him to yield:
But neither prayers could prevail, nor wishes,
Then I resolved to kill him—even with kisses.

Afraid, he fled then in her eyes to hide him;
   Out of her eyes into her lips again.
Stay, fond wretch, stay; thus I begun to chide him;
   Or choose her heart—thou changest oft in vain:
So, as by thee our lips else are united,
Our hearts, also, to join may be invited.

But nothing could the cruel spider move,
   To leave his hold, delighting in my woe;
She likewise, whom I served, but scorn'd my love,
   Laughing to see my trickling tears down go:
The more she did perceive increase my pain,
The more she match'd my love with cold disdain.

What then, shall I leave off my hope to speed,
   And live no more cross'd with consuming care?
No! let her frown and flyte, there's no remead,—
   I live resolved never to despair:
Content I am, and so my faith deservest,
My spring be toilsome, with a pleasant harvest.

                           W. MUIRE—1611.

TO THE MOST HOPEFUL AND HIGH-BORN PRINCE,
CHARLES, PRINCE OF WALES. [CHARLES I.]

MATCHLESS Montgomery in his native tongue,
In former times to thy great SIRE hath sung;
And often ravish'd his harmonious ear,
With strains fit only for a prince to hear.

My muse, which nought doth challenge worthy fame,
Save from MONTGOMERY she her birth doth claim
(Although his Phœnix' ashes have sent forth,
Pan for Apollo, if compared in worth),
Pretendeth title to supply his place,
By right hereditar to serve thy grace:
Though the puny issues of my weak engine,
Can add small lustre to thy glories shine,
Which like the boundless ocean swells no more,
Though springs and founts infuse their liquid store.
And though the gift be mean I may bestow,
Yet, gracious prince, my mite to thee I owe,
Which I with zeal present.   Oh deign to view
These artless measures, to thee only due.
  When thy ancestors' passions I have shown,
  If but[1] offence, great Charles, I'll sing thine own.

The most unworthy of your Highnesses vassals—S. W. M.

SIX LINES UPON THE FALL OF SOMERSET.

EACH man with silence stops his mouth, and hears
Sad news with wonder; but my barren muse
Fain would burst forth, but yet to write forbears:
Fear to offend must be my best excuse.
Since malice thirsts for brave Ephestion's blood,
I'll write no ill, nor dare I write no good.

1616.

1 i. e. without: we have invariably retained the word, where it occurs
in this sense.

SIX LINES SENT TO ME BY MY COUSIN,

MR. W. MUIR.

ARE lofty Parnassus' sacred shades disdain'd,
Though Hymen, Sir, hath clipp'd your wanton wings?
Ah! hearken how your proud Apollo plain'd—
That now no Orpheus strains his golden strings.
Shall saffron shirt, for his most glorious bay,
In willow boughs, make you, so cease your lay?

A REPROACH TO THE PRATTLER.

ENVIOUS wretch! on earth the most ingrate,
    In Venus' court thy liberty is losed,
Deserving punishment as Momus' mait,
    Misconstruing ladies merrily disposed!
If proud Ixion, in the hells inclosed,
    Doth suffer torture on the restless wheel—
Justly from all felicity deposed,
    Juno's discredit who did not conceal.
And if Acteon Cynthia's ire did feel,
    Turn'd in a hart—thus for a view revenged—
Much more thou, then, who ladies did reveal,
    In worse than he demerits to be changed:
Form'd in a dog, to bark at such most meet,
As chamber-talk divulges on the street!

Finis—1614.

"CHAUNSOUNE."

CALLING to mind the heavenly feature,
  The bashful blinks and comely grace,
  The form of her angelic face,
Deck'd with the quintessence of nature;
  To none inferior in place:
        Oft am I forced,
        Although divorced
    From presence of my dearest's eyes,
        The too slow day,
        To steal away
    Admiring her, my smart who sees.

Although she, ruthless she, doth know
  The secret burden of my woes,
  The tears which from mine eyes down goes—
Regretting Fortune, now my foe,
  In whom much once I did repose:
        Yet she, alace!
        Cares not my case;
    No spates of tears her heart can move:
        She knows my pain,
        Yet doth disdain;
    But, woe's me, I must still her love.

Though by mine eyes I should distil
  And quite dissolve in tears my heart,
  To satisfy her causeless smart;
Yet, rather she delights to kill,
  Than any joy to me impart.

But since the Fates,
Who rules all states,
Such tragic luck to me doth threat,
Do what she can,
Resolv'd I am,
To love her more than she can hate.

Although she frown, shall I despair;
Or, if it please her, prove unkind,
Shall I abstract my loyal mind?
Oh no! it's she must hale my sair;
For her, I loath not to be pined.
She, I suppose,
Like to the rose,
The prick before the smell imparts:
Heart breaking woes
Oft times foregoes
The mirth of mourning, martyr'd hearts.

Finis—WILLIAM MUIR—1611.

A REPLY to "I CARE NO WHETHER I GET HER OR NO."

To plead but where mutual kindness is gain'd,
And fancy only where favour hath place;
Such frozen affection I ever disdain'd,
Can ought be impair'd by distance or space.
My love shall be endless where once I affect—
Even though it should please her my service reject:
Still shall I determine, till breath and life go,
To love her whether she love me or no.

If she, by whose favour I live, should disdain,
   Shall I match her unkindness by proving ingrate?
Oh no! in her keeping my heart must remain—
   To honour and love her more than she can hate.
Her pleasure can no ways return to my smart,
Whose life in her power, must stay or depart:
   Though fortune delight in my overthrow,
   I'll love her whether she love me or no.

To lose both travel and time for a frown,
   And change for a secret surmise of disdain;
Love's force, and true virtue, to such is unknown,
   Whose faintness of courage is constancy's stain.
My loyal affection no time shall diminish;
Where once I affect, my favour shall finish:
   So shall I determine, till breath and life go,
   To love her whether she love me or no.

             Finis—*October* 10, 1614.

FAIR GODDESS, LOADSTAR OF DELIGHT.

To the Tune of "PERT JEAN."

FAIR goddess! loadstar of delight,
   Nature's triumph, and beauty's life,
Earth's ornament, my hope's full height;
   My only peace, and pleasing strife!
Let mercy mollify thy mind—
   A Saturn's heart, should Venus have?
Or, should thou prove to him unkind,
   Who humbly life of thee doth crave?

Since all thy parts some special grace
Decoirs, to show thy heavenly race,
Virtue thy mind, and love thy face,
　　Proportion brave thy feature:
Pity then, must needs have place
　　In such a divine creature,
　　　　Whose sweetness,
　　　　And meekness,
Exceeds the bounds of nature!

When first those angel's eyes I view'd,
　　Two sparks to inflame a world of love—
My fatal thraldom then ensued;
　　Then did my liberty remove.
There, first, infected was my mind;
　　Love's nectared poison there I drank—
Thy sacred countenance aye shined
　　So far above all human rank.
Let then those eyes, which did ensnare,
Those shining stars, their fault repair;
Dispensing, by their beams preclair,
　　The clouds of thy disdaining.
Wisdom, virtue, beauty rare,
　　In thee have all remaining.
　　　　Let not then,
　　　　The sport then,
Of rigour, be thy staining.

Should cruelty, sweet love, eclipse
　　The sunshine of those glorious rays?
Or, should those lovely smiling lips
　　Breathe forth affection's delays?

M

Let mercy countervail thy worth,
 And measure pity by my pain,
So, thy perfections to paint forth,
 An endless labour shall remain.
Let beauty's beams then thaw away,
Reflecting only on us tway,
The iciness of love's delay;
 And melt disdain's cold treasure.
Nature's due so shall we pay,
 Bathing in boundless pleasure;
  Enjoying,
  And toying,
Whose sweets exceed all measure.

Finis—1615, W. M. Rowallan.

NO CHANGE SHALL PART MY LOVE AND ME.
To the Tune of "ANE NEW LILT."

BEAUTY hath mine eyes assail'd,
 And subdued my soul's affection;
Cupid's dart hath so prevail'd,
 That I must live in his subjection.
Tied till one who's matchless alone,
And second to none in all perfection:
 Since my fortune such must be,
 No change shall part my love and me!

Wisdom, meekness, virtue, grace,
 Sweetness, modesty, bounty, but measure,
Decks her sweet celestial face—
 Rich in beauty's heavenly treasure.

Joy, nor smart, shall never divert,
My most loyal heart, for pain nor pleasure:
    But, resolved, I avow, till I die,
    No change shall part my love and me!

Time, nor distance, shall have force,
    Although by fortune's smile invited,
Us two ever to divorce!
    By such a sympathy united.
True love hates the wavering estates,
Of such as the Fates hath changed or retreated!
    But recourse, in any degree,
    No change shall part my love and me!

Dear! let death then only finish,
    And alter alone our choice and election;
Let no change our love diminish,
    Nor breed from constancy any defection.
Time nor space, no distance of place,
Shall ever deface our fervent affection.
    Then, sweet love! thus let us decree,
    No change shall part us while we die.

                        Finis—1615.

At the date of these fervent verses, the author, for the first time, had entered the holy bands of matrimony; so, the object of his present devotions can hardly be mistaken. They are, probably,

      A *copy*, and no more,
      Of something better, seen before.

SONNETS.

MORE chaste than fair Diana, first in place;
  From whose fair eyes flows love's alluring springs;
Second to none in bounty, beauty grace,
  Whose heavenly hands holds proud Cupid's stings.
Endless report, upon aspiring wings,
  Thy high heroic virtues hath stored;
Admired, but maik, even in a thousand things:
  To eternize thee Fame hath endeavor'd.
Miraculous, matchless Margarite! decoir'd
  With all preferments nature can afford;
Favour'd from heavens above, on earth adored!
  Extoll'd by truth of thy most loyal word.
With virtue graced far more than form of face,
Yet Venus, in the same, doth yield thee place.

MAIR GRAIT than I can any ways deserve,
  Mair rair than fair, yet matchless in the same;
Who with thy eyes, least my poor life should starve,
  Vouchsafes to look with pity on my pain.
Here, I avow, thine ever to remain,
  To serve thee still, till breath and life depart,
Revived by virtue of thy sacred name:
  Come death or life, in love I find no smart.
Let Cupid wreck him on my martyr'd heart,
  Let fortune frown, and all the world envy,
If I be thine, no grief can death impart,
  Shall make me seem thy service to deny.
I live mair weil contended thine to die,
Than crown'd with honour and disdain'd by thee.

CAN any cross, shall ever intervene,
  Make me to change my never-changing mind?
Can ought that my poor eyes hath ever seen
  Make me to her, who holds my life, unkind?
O no! even though the world's beauty shined,
  To try my truth, and tempt my loyal love;
I more esteem for her to live still pined
  Than any other, be preferr'd above.
My constant heart no torture shall remove:
  Though duilful death, and frowning fortune threat,
No grief at all, no pain that I can prove,
  Shall make me ever loathe of my estate.
I gladly yield me, let her save or kill—
I hate to live except it be her will.

ALACE! sweet love, that ever my poor eyes
  Presum'd to gaze on that most heavenly face!
Alace! that fortune ever seem'd to ease
  My endless woes, but now would me deface.
Alace! that ever I expected grace;
  To snare myself, in hope to be relieved!
Alace! alace! that Love would now disgrace
  My loyal heart, which once to serve him lived!
Alace! alace! that ever I survived
  The fatal time, when first appear'd my joy:
For now, alace, I die: but yet revived
  In hope, thy love my luck shall once enjoy.
Still to remain, resolved then shall I live,
Thy humble servant, even till breath me leave!

Thir Sonets, maid 1612.

We have been able to obtain no revealings whatever of the particular object of our author's inspiration, and "pleasant dying," so ardently breathed forth in the four preceding Sonnets.   However viewed by modern critics, such seems the almost invariable style of Rowallan's musings: and but rarely, if indeed ever, seems he to have devoted them to other than the two grand concernments—religion and love.   The three succeeding should possibly still be viewed as a continuation of the same subject; in its scope, the concluding Sonnet seems a little more general.

SONNETS.

Like as Acteon found the fatal bounds,
  Whereas Diana bath'd her by a well;
Which high attempt—punish'd by his own hounds—
  Turn'd in a timorous hart, he fled, but fell.
So while my Cynthia, who doth her excel,
  I did behold cruel Cupid envied,
And mine own eyes to cross me did compel,—
  Still gazing on the goddess they espied.
At liberty before, alace! now tied,
  I live expecting my Diana's doom—
Either to be preferr'd, or die denied!
  Unworthy of the honour to presume.
Yet, though I die—for so I ever do—
Had I more lives, them should I hazard too.

Finis—1612.

Adieu, my love, my life, my bliss, my being!
  My hope, my hap, my joy, my all, adieu!
Adieu, sweet subject of my pleasant dying,
  And most delightful object of my view!

Bright spark of beauty! paragon'd by few;
　　Unspotted pearl! which doth thy sex adorn;
Loadstar of love! whose pure vermilion hue,
　　Makes pale the rose, and stains the blushing morn!
That zeal to thee which I have ever borne,
　　Sole essence, life, and vigour of my spreit!
By track of time shall never be outworn:
　　My second self, my charming Syren sweet!
And so, my Phœnix and my turtle true,
A thousand thousand times adieu, adieu!

　　　　　　　W. M. ROWALLANE, Younger, 1615.

SOME gallant spirits, desirous of renown,
　　To climb, with pain, Parnassus do aspire:
By nature some do wear the laurel crown,
　　And some the poet proves for hope of hire!
But none of those my spirits doth inspire;
　　My Muse is more admired than all the Nine,
Who doth infuse my breast with sacred fire,
　　To paint *her* forth most heavenly and divine!
Her worth I raise in elegiac line,
　　In lyrics sweet, her beauties I extol,
The brave heroic doth her rare ingine
　　In time's immortal register enrol.
Since thou of me hath made thy poet then,
Be bold, sweet lady, to employ my pen!

　　　　　　　Finis—1616.

In beauty, love's sweet object, ravish'd sight,
   Doth some peculiar perfection prize,
   In which most worth and admiration lies;
   The senses charming with most dear delight:
Some eyes adore like stars, clear, glist'ring, bright;
   Some, wrapp'd in black those comets most entice;
   Some are transported with pureayn dyes,[1]
   And some most value green about the light.
Aurora's flaming hair some fondly love;
   White dangling tresses—yellow curls of gold,
   Others in greatest estimation hold:
   All eyes alike,—each beauty doth not move.
Eyes lovely brown, brown chesnut-colour'd hair,
Inflame *my* heart, and senses all ensnare.

TUA SONETS SENT BY MY FREIND, A. S.

Thou kno's, braue gallant, that our Scottich braines
   Hawe ay bein England's equals ewery way;
Quhair als rair muse, and martiall myndis remaines,
   With als renouned records to this day.
Thoght we be not enrol'd so rich as they,
   Yit haue we wits of worth enrich'd more rare:
As for thair Sidneyes science, qubich they say,
   Surpasseth all in his Arcadian air,—
Cum, I haue found our westerne feelds als fair;
   Go thou to work, and I schall be thy guyde,
And schew the of a sueitar subject thair—
   Borne Beuties wonder on the banks of Clyd!
Philocle and Pamela, those sueit twain,
Quho lake bot thee to eternize thair name.

---

1 Purple, or blue.

PLAY thou the Sidney to thy native soyle,

   And rousse thy silwer pen, yat sleept this quhyle,

And spair not for thy tyme-beguyling toyle;

   Nor spend thy gallant spirit in exyle!

For first, thou art ane Lower by thy style,

   Then borne ane Westerne, quhair those Ladyes wse,—

And they the only object of this Ile—

   Quhoise rair renouned worth I kna thou lowse,

May moue thee as thair Champioun, quhom they chuse,

   To cheir thy braines and grace tham with the best.

Sprang thou from Maxwell and Montgomeries muse?

   To let our poets perisch in the West!

No, no! braue youth, continow in thy kynd,

No sueitar subject sall thy Muses fynd! ·

Of the author of these spirited lines, there appears no clearer intelligence than what the prefixed initials afford. However, they were probably written about the year 1617; and in some editions of the Sempills of Beltrees' contemporary satire of the *Packman and the Priest,* appears a not unequal sonnet ascribed to an *Alexander Sempill:* if correct, possibly a son or near relation of the family, and it may be, the writer of these laudatory verses addressed to our author.

The name of *Maxwell,* which here occurs as a then recognised poet, has perhaps perished! The relation, however, assigned him to Sir W. Mure, whose grandmother was a daughter of Maxwell of New-wark, Renfrewshire, would seem pretty certainly to indicate his descent from that branch of the Maxwells. Almost nothing, indeed, seems known of the history of poetry in the West Lowlands of Scotland. And it is pleasing to learn, Mr. Motherwell of Paisley purposes soon to supply an entire and creditable edition of the poetical writings of the Sempills of Beltrees above alluded to, with memoirs of that interesting and very remarkable family.

The orthography of these two Sonnets, and of the Epitaphs which follow, has carefully been preserved as in the original papers. Small thanks, we are aware, must be due to us by the antiquary, for the pains we have taken to conform the preceding portion of these selections, to the spelling of the present day; but in a compilation more intended for ordinary than antiquarian use, such an alteration seemed somewhat imperious. This, however, is the utmost license which has been taken, as, we think, the critical reader will easily be satisfied of.

THE EPITAPH

OF THE RYT. VENERABLE GODLY AND LEARNED FATHER GEORGE, BE GRACE FROM GOD ORDERLY CALLIT, AND BE HIS PRINCE APOYNTED TO BE GREATEST PRELATE IN SCOTLAND, ARCHBISCHOPE OF SANCT-ANDROIS, &c.

BEREFT of breath, yit nocht from lyfe depoised,
  Heir lyes inclosid Sanctandrois richest treassour:
A pearle but meassour hath ye wordill loossed,
  Quhoise mynd repoissed in no decaying pleassour.
A matchles Phœnix, quho from mein estait,
Becam a Prelat and a Prince's mait.

A painfull Pastour, worthy such a place;
  Too schort a space his natioune hath decoired;
Quho now, restored to earth, doth rest in peace;
  Receaued in grace, the heawinis in Sanctis hath stoired:
Quhoise corpis t'intomb, glaid ar ye sensles stones,
Promou'd to honour by his buried bones.

In Zoilum.

Thou then, quho by thy false and fcnzied fact,
Strywes to detract this prudent Prelat's name,
Bewar such schame becum thy suirest hap,
Thrawin from ye tap of fortoune to defame.
No blot, no blemisch, no defect, no moth
Presum'd to enter in so rich a cloth!

ANE EPITAPH

EFTER YE VULGAR OPINIOUNE WPON YE DEATH OF GEORGE GLAID-
STANES, B. OF S. A.

GLAIDSTANES is gone! his corpis doth heir duell,
Bot quhair be his oyer halfe, no man can tell:
The heauinis doth abhor to ludge such a ghost,
Quho still quhill he liued to Pluto raid post;
The earth hath expell'd him, as loathing such load,
Quho honoured Bacchus and no other god.
Since both then reiect him, t' this outcast of heavin
In midst of ye Furies a place must be giwin:
Quhose covetouse mynd no richesse contented,
Bot heiping wp treassour wnmyndful quho lent it;
Till contrary fortoun, by turning ye dyce,
Metamorphos'd his *thousands* in millions of lyce!
Quhich endit ye dayes of this sensuall slave—
Wnwordy the earth sould yeild him a grave!

By him quho wischeth, that this wretches fait
May giwe exemple wnto ewery stait:
That hyer powares be with feir regairdit;
Or, by this Athist's punischment rewairded!

Finis—1615.

These curious verses would seem at least a not unapt comment on the conflicting rancour of the period to which they belong; and so far may apologise for their present appearance.

George Gladstanes, the prelate to whom they appear to relate, was advanced to the metropolitan see of St. Andrews in 1606, and died in the incumbency, May 2, 1615. "He was son of Halbert Gladstanes, Clerk of Dundee; and had his education in the Latin there. He seems to have brought on his own death upon himself, by indulging his appetite. He lived a filthy belly-god; he died of a filthy and loathsome disease, σκωληχο βρωτος." *Wodrow MS. in Bib. Col. Glas.* where other epitaphs on the same prelate, of no higher delicacy, and certainly not less virulent, are recorded.

Spotswood, who ran perhaps as high on the opposite side, though doubtless somewhat more tempered, characterises the archbishop as "a man of good learning, ready utterance, and great invention; but of an easy nature, and induced by those he trusted, to do many things hurtful to the see."

Three other Epitaphs occur in the MSS. one on the "Lady Arnestoun," 1616; and another, dated 1617, is inscribed to the memory of the "Laird of Arnestoun, youngar;"—of both, the poet has to deplore their "vntymelie fait." The third Epitaph, which want of room alone precludes being now printed, is dated 1614; and records the premature death of the "excellent gentil-uoman A. C. [Agnes Cuningham] sister to ye Laird of Caprin-toun," Ayrshire.

Overtoun, July, 1827.

SECTION III.

SONGS AND BALLADS,

TRADITIONAL AND SELECTED.

BALLADS AND SONGS,

TRADITIONAL AND SELECTED.

LORD DELAWARE.

IN the Parliament House,
 A great rout has been there,
Betwixt our good King
 And the Lord Delaware:
Says Lord Delaware
 To his Majesty full soon,
Will it please you, my Liege,
 To grant me a boon?

What's your boon, says the King,
 Now let me understand?
It's, give me all the poor men
 We've starving in this land;
And without delay, I'll hie me
 To Lincolnshire,
To sow hemp-seed and flax-seed,
 And hang them all there.

For with hempen cord its better
 To stop each poor man's breath,
Than with famine you should see
 Your subjects starve to death.
Up starts a Dutch Lord,
 Who to Delaware did say,
Thou deservest to be stabb'd!
 Then he turn'd himself away:

Thou deservest to be stabb'd,
 And the dogs have thine ears,
For insulting our King
 In this Parliament of peers;
Up sprang a Welsh Lord,
 The brave Duke of Devonshire,
In young Delaware's defence, I'll fight
 This Dutch Lord, my Sire.

For he is in the right,
 And I'll make it so appear:
Him I dare to single combat,
 For insulting Delaware.
A stage was soon erected,
 And to combat they went,
For to kill, or to be kill'd,
 It was either's full intent.

But the very first flourish,
 When the heralds gave command,
The sword of brave Devonshire
 Bent backward on his hand;

In suspense he paused awhile,
   Scann'd his foe before he strake,
Then against the king's armour,
   His bent sword he brake.

Then he sprang from the stage,
   To a soldier in the ring,
Saying, "Lend your sword, that to an end
   This tragedy we bring:
Though he's fighting me in armour,
   While I am fighting bare,
Even more than this I'd venture,
   For young Lord Delaware."

Leaping back on the stage,
   Sword to buckler now resounds,
Till he left the Dutch Lord
   A bleeding in his wounds:
This seeing, cries the King
   To his guards without delay,
"Call Devonshire down,—
   Take the dead man away!"

No, says brave Devonshire,
   I've fought him as a man,
Since he's dead, I will keep
   The trophies I have won;
For he fought me in your armour,
   While I fought him bare,
And the same you must win back, my Liege,
   If ever you them wear.

God bless the Church of England,
　　May it prosper on each hand,
And also every poor man
　　Now starving in this land;
And while I pray success may crown
　　Our king upon his throne,
I'll wish that every poor man,
　　May long enjoy his own.

An imperfect copy of the foregoing interesting Ballad, was noted down by us from the singing of a gentleman in this city, which has necessarily been re-modelled and smoothed down to the present measure, without any other liberties, however, having been taken with the original narrative, which is here carefully preserved as it was committed to us, while the spirit of our original, so far as our endeavours were competent for the task, has been retained throughout. We have not, as yet, been able to trace out the historical incident upon which the Ballad appears to have been founded, yet those curious in such matters may consult, if they list, "Proceedings and Debates in the House of Commons, for 1621 and 1622," where they will find that some stormy debatings in these several years, have been agitated in Parliament regarding the Corn Laws, which bear pretty close upon the leading features of the above. The air is beautiful, and peculiar to the Ballad.

THE BONNY LASS O' GOWRIE.

A wee bit north frae yon green wood,
　　Whare draps the sunny showerie,
The lofty elm-trees spread their boughs,
　　To shade the braes o' Gowrie;
An' by yon burn ye scarce can see,
　　There stan's a rustic bowerie,
Whare lives a lass mair dear to me,
　　Than a' the maids in Gowrie.

Nae gentle bard e'er sang her praise,
   'Cause fortune ne'er left dowrie;
The rose blaws sweetest in the shade,
   So does the flower o' Gowrie.
When April strews her garlands roun',
   She barefoot treads the flowrie;
Her sang gars a' the woodlands ring,
   That shade the braes o' Gowrie.

Her modest blush an' downcast e'e,
   A flame sent beating through me;
For she surpasses all I've seen,
   This peerless flower o' Gowrie.
I've lain upon the dewy green
   Until the evening hourie,
An' thought 'gin ere I durst ca' mine,
   The bonnie lass o' Gowrie.

The bushes that o'erhang the burn,
   Sae verdant an' sae flowerie,
Can witness that I love alane,
   The bonnie lass o' Gowrie.
Let ithers dream, an' sigh for wealth,
   An' fashions fleet an' flowery,
Gie me that hamely innocence
   Upon the braes o' Gowrie.

Revised from an old stall copy, which ascribes the composition
of the original Ballad to a COL. JAMES RAMSAY of Stirling Castle.

THE EWE LAMB.

I'LL gie thee jewels, an' I'll gie thee rings,
I'll gie thee pearls, an' many fine things,
I'll gie thee silk petticoats fringed to the knee,
If thou'lt lea'e father an' mother, an' marry wi' me.

I'll nane o' your jewels, I'll nane o' your rings,
I'll nane o' your pearlings nor ither fine things,
Nor skyrin silk petticoats fringed to the knee,
But I'll lea' father an' mother, an' marry wi' thee.

But my father's a shepherd, wi' his flocks on yon hill,
Ye may gang to the auld man, an' ask his gude-will:
Indeed will I, Jeanie, an' bring answer to thee,
Sae, amang the berry-bushes 'gin gloamin meet me.

Good-morrow, old father! ye're feeding your flock;
Will you grant me a ewe-lamb to bring up a stock?
Indeed will I, Jamie, says he, frank an' free:
Sae, amang the berrie-bushes, my Jeanie met me.

How blyth look'd young Jamie, as he took her by the hand,
Syne up before the old man this young couple stand;
Says, this is the ewe-lamb that I ask'd of thee,
'Twas amang the berry-bushes this young thing met me.

O foul fa' thee, Jamie, thou hast me beguil'd,
I little thought the ewe-lamb thou ask'd was my child;
But since it is sae, that in love you agree,
My blessing gang wi' ye, my dochter, quoth he.

The foregoing Pastoral is noted down from recitation; one or two of the intermediate stanzas appear to be common with the North-country Ballad of the " Laird of Drum." The air is sweetly plaintive, and peculiar to itself.

THE YOUNG MAN'S DREAM.

WHEN wint'ry storms keep yelling round,
By the blazing hearth we are oftenest found;
But in summer, when the fields are dry,
To the hunting goes my dog and I.

As my dog and I went down yon glen,
I smiled to a maiden who smiled again,
As tripping lightly o'er the bent,
To milk her ewes by the bughts she went.

O maiden mine, I have dream'd a dream;
Beneath the storm and the lightning's gleam,
I seem'd to lean on this branching oak,
When the black clouds met, and the tempest broke

Above my lorn head, and fired the tree,
Where, chill'd and trembling thou clung by me;
Oh! deep and deathlike was thy swoon,
As the thunders peal'd, and the rains fell down.

Some kinder rain-drops than the rest,
On thy lily brow and scarce heaving breast,
Fell pattering down, and the deep swoon broke—
With a sigh and shiver, to life thou woke.

I kiss'd the cold drops off, one by one,
Till thou gazed on me as the sun
Burst through, and chased the dense clouds away,
And the closed flowers spread to the sunny day.

She smiled, and said, " When you dream again,
Some fairer vision may change your strain;
And wealth and beauty may meet your view—
So begone, young man, for I love not you:

I love no pears, I love no plums,
Nor dreams that fade when the morning comes;
But I love the cherry that grows on yon tree,
So does my true-love, where'er he be."

A few lines of " The Young Man's Dream," are adopted from
an old free traditional Ballad, that has nearly faded from our recollection; while the rest is original.   The air is common with a
good many of our West-country chaunts of the same measure.

THE SWAIN'S RESOLVE.

I once lov'd a maid, though she slighted me,
    Because I had lately grown poor;
And she stole, before I wist it, my poor heart away,
    And she'll keep it for ever more.

I went to my love's chamber-door one night,
    And I knock'd, her favour to win;
Without doubt my love arose, and slipp'd on her clothes,
    Ere she came down to let me in.

As soon as I saw my true-love's face,
   My heart grew light and fain,
And I clasp'd her round the middle so small,
   And kiss'd the dear maid again.

She cries to the cock, saying, thou must not crow,
   Until that the day be worn;
And thy wings shall be made of the silvery gray,
   And thy voice of the silver horn.

As homeward I hied o'er yon lofty hill,
   The wind it blew high and cold,
Then I wish'd I were safe by my true-love's side again,
   Her fair form once more to enfold.

———

Oh I'll be as constant to my true love,
   As the dial is to the sun;
And if she will not be the very same to me,
   She is far better lost than won.

Noted down partly from recollection, but chiefly from the recitation of the gentleman who has favoured us with the Ballads of
Lord Delaware, and the Ewe Lamb. The air is peculiarly lively
and beautiful, and well merits preservation; which, along with
the Ballad itself, seems peculiar to Ayrshire; and, so far as we
are aware, neither the one nor the other have ever yet been committed to paper. The fourth stanza here, appears in common with
one in the "Gray Cock," "Saw ye my Father," &c.; in other
points the twain are different, whilst their respective melodies are
altogether dissimilar.

THE MILK MAIDS' REQUEST.

THREE maidens a-milking did go,
Three maidens a-milking did go,
    The wind it blew high,
    And the wind it blew low,
Which tossed their pails to and fro.

They met a young swain whom they knew,
They met a young swain that they knew,
    They asked of him
    If he had any skill,
How to catch them a small bird or two.

O yes, I have very good skill,
O yes, I've got very good skill,
    If you'll go along with me,
To the bonnie green-wood tree,
I will catch you a bird to your will.

To the merry green-wood as they went,
To the merry green-wood as they went,
    The small birds were singing
    Upon ilka green tree,
While the gay rose above the lily bent.

———

Ripe berries are soft to the touch,
Ripe berries are soft to the touch,
    And the birds of a feather,
    They will all flock together,
Let the people say little or much.

From recollection;—air plaintive and pastoral.

BILLY BOY.

MAN the boat, all hands aboard, Billy boy, Billy boy,
Mark the signal, hands aboard, Billy boy, ·
      Each moving, thrilling word,
      As I steer from my adored
Lovely Nancy, says thy fancy, lingers round thy darling boy.

Is the maid so dear to thee, Billy boy, Billy boy?
Is her heart with thee at sea, Billy boy?
      The maid is dear to me,
      As the bark is to the tree,
Since my Nancy won my fancy, I'm her darling Billy boy.

Worth and merit bids thee prove, Billy boy, Billy boy,
If she's meet to be thy love, Billy boy;
      She's as meet to be my love,
      As the hand is for the glove,
Since my Nancy won my fancy, I'm her darling Billy boy.

Can the maid thou would'st adore, Billy boy, Billy boy,
Row or steer the boat ashore, Billy boy?
      She can row the boat ashore,
      With the paddle or the oar,
Thus my Nancy won my fancy, I'm her darling Billy boy.

Then a health to thine and thee, Billy boy, Billy boy,
We will pledge when on the sea, Billy boy;
      And when heaven wills again,
      Our return from o'er the main,
May thy Nancy find thy fancy still the same, my Billy boy.

In the foregoing attempt, we have taken the liberty of re-modelling and pruning the intermediate stanzas of an old free traditional Ballad, bearing the same choral terminations of "Billy boy;" while the first and concluding verses are necessarily original, by way of completing the chant. The air, tradition has attached to it, is peculiarly lively and spirit-stirring; and approaches pretty near that of our own Song, "Kelvin Grove," or, as an amateur would say, to an *ear-set* of "Robie dun a gorach."

POOR AULD MAIDENS.

THREE score and ten of us,
　　Poor auld maidens!
Three score and ten of us,
　　Poor auld maidens!
Three score and ten of us,
Lame, and blind, and comfortless,
Without a penny in our purse,
　　Poor auld maidens!

Yet we bear a willing mind,
　　Poor auld maidens!
Yet we bear a willing mind,
　　Poor auld maidens!
Yet we bear a willing mind,
If we a young man could but find,
For to kiss the lame and blind,
　　Nor die auld maidens.

Oh but young men are unco nice,
　　Poor auld maidens!

Oh but young men are unco nice,
 Poor auld maidens!
Oh but young men are unco nice,
And auld men's offers we despise;
Oh! we'll get leave to shut our eyes,
 An' die auld maidens.

But oh! gin we were young again,
 Poor auld maidens!
But oh! gin we were young again,
 Poor auld maidens!
But oh! gin we were young again,
We nae mair would lie our lane,
For we despise the scornfu' name
 O' poor auld maidens!

Noted down from the singing of a Lady, we never having met
with the original in print. The modern song of " Nice Young
Maidens" has doubtlessly been metaphrased from the above. The
air is a tolerable one of its class, lively, and peculiar to the Ballad.

THE AULD WIFE O' LAUDERDALE.

IN Lauderdale there lived a wife,
 As canty a carline's ever was seen;
Her gudeman began to drap wi' age,
 While she was rosy, fresh, an' green:
The auld wife in Lauderdale,
The queer auld wife in Lauderdale;
At forty she had tooth and nail,
The canty auld wife o' Lauderdale.

She growl'd on Tammie day an' night,
　An' wonder'd aye that he should fail;
An' ca'd him syne a silly wight,
　Else he might cast anither spale:
The auld wife in Lauderdale,
The queer auld wife in Lauderdale;
She thought that Tammie never should fail!
The rosy auld wife in Lauderdale.

Youth, health, and strength are dauntless chiels,
　When they in a' their vigour shine;
But hirplin' hostin' age comes on,
　An' fun and frolics maun decline:
This ken'd the man in Lauderdale,
The douse auld man o' Lauderdale;
He fan' his strength beginning to fail,
An' parts to cool in Lauderdale.

A wonder-working doctor cam'
　To Dunse, wha' cured the blin' an' lame;
She ran to Dunse withouten fail,
　To ease her pains in Lauderdale:
I've come this day frae Lauderdale,
I'm sure ye've heard o' Lauderdale,
O' ilka place it is the wale,
The sweet an' pleasant Lauderdale.

O doctor, doctor, tent my moan,
　I maun tell you a mournfu' tale:
My Tammie's auld an' cauldrife grown,
　While I am blooming fresh and hale;

O wad ye come to Lauderdale,
Ye maun come east to Lauderdale;
An' pass your skill on Tammie's ail,
The sleepy auld man o' Lauderdale.

I wauk a' night, an' sleep get nane,
   While he is snoring soun' an' leal;
I might as weel lie by a stane,
   Or ony rotten auld fir dail:
I've weary nights in Lauderdale,
I sigh an' sab in Lauderdale;
Now ye'll hae medicine, I'se be bail,
To ease our waes in Lauderdale.

O ay, the doctor smiling said,
   I think that I cou'd cure your ail;
But ye maun change auld Tammie's food,
   To birsled pease, an' butter'd ale:
Birsled pease in Lauderdale,
Butter'd ale in Lauderdale;
Gie Tammie that at ilka meal,
'Twill cheer his auld heart in Lauderdale.

The auld wife now gaed cantie hame,
   Sae gleg an' donsie o'er the dale;
And pray'd and wis'd that Tammie's teeth
   Would maup the pease in Lauderdale:
Birsled pease in Lauderdale,
Quo' the snod auld wife o' Lauderdale;
I wis' and houp our Tammie's teeth
May crack the pease in Lauderdale.

Now a' ye wives baith far and near,
   Whenever your men begin to fail;
Ye needna' youk, an' growl, an' ban,
   Do like the carline in Lauderdale:
Butter'd ale in Lauderdale,
Birsled pease in Lauderdale;
A peck o' pease will cure your ail,
It cured the auld man's in Lauderdale.

The foregoing spirited and graphic Ballad is noted down from recitation, we never having met with the original in print. The penultimate stanza, for the sake of connection, is original, as the one which stood in its place had escaped the memory of our fair minstrel.

UP WI' THE WIDOW.

WELCOME, my Johnny, beardless an' bonny,
Ye're my conceit, though I'm courted by mony;
Come to the spence, my ain merry ploughman,
Make it your hame, ye'll be baith het an' fu', man:
   Baith het an' fu', man, baith het an' fu', man,
   Make it your hame, ye'll be baith het an' fu', man.

Gin ye be tentie, ye shall hae plenty,
Year after year, I hae dotted a renty,
Byres fu' o' horse an' kye, barns fu' o' grain, man,
Bukes fu' o' notes, an' a farm o' your ain man;

At market or fair, man, ye may be there, man,
Buying or selling, wi' plenty to ware, man,
Dress'd like a laird, in the bravest an' warmest,
On a guide beast, you'll ride up wi' the foremost.

Taupie young lassies, keeking in glasses,
Wasting their siller on trinkets an' dresses,
Think wi' yoursel', Johnny tak wha ye may do,
Ye may do war than draw up wi' the widow,

   Up wi' the widow, up wi' the widow,

   Ye may do war than draw up wi' the widow.

This cleverly descriptive Song of its class, was several years
ago, noted down by us, from the singing of a lady. We never have
seen it in print, among the numerous Song collections turned
over in quest of it, nor ever since or before heard it sung; yet
from the perfect manner in which we found it, we do not think it
can be an old one, nor is the piece, for rustic humour, and paint-
ing, unworthy the pen of the Ettrick Shepherd himself.

WHEN I WAS YOUNG MAN.

WHEN I was a young man, O then, O then,
When I was a young man, O then,
   I'd a horse for to ride,
   With a sword by my side,
And the world it went rarely with me, then, O then,
O the world it went rarely with me, then.

I married a wife, O then, O then,
I married a wife, O then:

My saddle and my bridle
Turn'd to rocking a cradle,
And the world it went worse with me then, just then,
O the world it went worse with me then.

My wife she fell sick, O then, O then,
My wife she fell sick, O then,
    She droop'd, and fell sick,
    And a fever follow'd it,
So the world went poorly with me then, O then,
O the world it went poorly with me then.

My wife she did die, O then, just then
My poor wife did die, O then,
    I tried for to sigh
    As I found I could not cry,
Though the world went so ill with me then, just then,
Though the world went so ill with me then.

I buried my wife, O then, O then,
I buried my wife, O then,
    I laid her in her grave,
    And return'd brisk and brave,
For the world was before me, just then, even then,
The world was now before me, again.

As homeward I hied me, O then, O then,
I chanced for to spy me, just then,
    A young blooming lass,
    Who was viewing in her glass,
What a beauty I thought her just then, even then,
So my heart follow'd after, just then.

I married this maiden, O then, O then,
Old griefs were fast fading, just then,
    But soon she turn'd a sot,
    And lov'd her pipe and pot,
So I wish'd for my old wife, again, again,
O I wish'd my old wife back again.

So I went to her grave, O then, O then,
Past follies were now in their wane,
    I opened her coffin,
    And saw my wife laughing.
Now the world went so rarely with me then, O then,
As my old wife came home with me again.

However much the fastidious critic may be inclined to snarl upon perusing the above plainly told and probable tale (which is here taken down from recitation), we cannot help thinking that it possesses some little merits in its own way, and also that it is worthy of preservation. The ditty itself is old, whilst the melody is brisk and lively; the original tune, we think, is to be found in Ravenscroft's "Melismata," air 19th, "Country Rounds:"

    " As I went by the way, holom, trolom,
    There I met by the way, hazom," &c.

I AM TOO YOUNG.

As I went out on a May morning,
    A May morning it happened to be;
Then I was aware of a weel-far't lass,
    Coming linkin over the lea to me;

She had a voice that was more clear, ..
 Than any damsel's under the sun;
I asked at her if she'd marry me?
 But her answer it was, "I am too young:"

"I am too young; with you to wed
 It would bring shame to all my kin,
So begone young man, and trouble me no more,
 For you never shall my favour win."
I took her by the lily-white hand,
 Aboon our heads the lavrocks sung;
Syne kiss'd her cherry cheeks and mou',
 And told her she was not a day too young.

Her colour came, her colour went—
 Awa frae me, the damsel sprung
With colly o'er the gowany bent,
 While in my ear her sweet voice voice rung,
Saying, " As I maut, sae maun I brew,
 And as I brew, sae maun I tun,
Gae tell your tale to some other fair May,
 For to marry with you, I am too young."

This Ballad in its original dress, at one time, we recollect, was
not only extremely popular, but a great favourite amongst the
young peasantry in the West of Scotland. To suit the times,
however, we have been necessitated to throw out the intermediate
stanzas, as their freedom would not bear transcription, while the
second and third verses have been slightly altered from the recited
copy. In the 4th volume of Johnston's Museum, another version
of it will be found, also a metaphrase from the same in volume
second of Cunningham's " Songs of Scotland." The air, tradition
affixes to it, is lively and peculiar to itself, and certainly merits
to be revived again.

THE WAKERIFE MAMMY.

As I gaed o'er the Highland hills,
    I met a bonnie lassie;
Wha' look'd at me, and I at her,
    And O but she was saucy.

Whare are ye gaun, my bonnie lass,
    Whare are ye gaun, my lammy;
Right saucily she answer'd me,
    An errand to my mammy.

An' whare live ye, my bonnie lass,
    Whare do ye won, my lammy;
Right modestly she answer'd me,
    In a wee cot wi' my mammy.

Will ye tak' me to your wee house,
    I'm far frae hame, my lammy;
Wi' a leer o' her eye, she answer'd me,
    I darna for my mammy.

But I fore up the glen at e'en,
    To see this bonnie lassie;
And lang before the gray morn cam',
    She wasna' half sae saucie.

O weary fa' the wakerife cock,
    An' the fumart lay his crawing;
He wauken'd the auld wife frae her rest,
    A wee blink or the dawing.

Wha straught began to blaw the coal,
　　To see gif she could ken me;
But I crap out from whare I lay,
　　And took the fields to skreen me.

———

She took her by the hair o' the head,
　　As frae the spence she brought her,
An' wi' a gude green hazel wand,
　　She's made her a weel paid dochter.

Now fare thee weel, my bonnie lass,
　　An fare thee weel, my lammy,
Tho' thou has a gay, an' a weel-far't face,
　　Yet thou has a wakerife mammy.

The "Wakerife mammy," is here noted down with some trifling corrections, from the west country set of the Ballad, where its day of popularity amongst the peasantry, was equal, at least, with that of the foregoing one. Burns says that he picked up a version of it from a country girl's singing in Nithsdale, and that he never either met with the song or the air to which it is sung elsewhere in Scotland. We marvel not a little at this, after considering how very common the Ballad has been over the shires of Ayr and Renfrew, both before and since the Poet's day; so common, indeed, is it still, that we have had some demurings about inserting it here at all. The air is a very pretty one, with two lines of a nonsensical chorus, sung after each stanza, which certainly merits other verses to be adapted for it, when like many other wanderers of the day, it then might again be received into favour. Burns's copy, in Johnston's Museum, differs a good deal from the foregoing one, besides wanting the commencing stanza. Cunningham's set of words in the second volume of his "Songs of Scotland," is equally faulty.

THE DESPONDING MAIDEN.

As Jockie was trudging the meadows along,
   So blythsome, so cheerful, and gay,
He happen'd to meet a young girl by the way,
   And her face it was o'ercover'd with care,
   And her face it was o'ercover'd with care.

He asked the maiden what made her so sad,
   Said, 'twas pity that she should complain;
She told him, she had lost her very best lad,
   And she ne'er would behold him again,
   No, she ne'er would behold him again.

Come dry up your tears, and no longer do mourn,
   Said Jockie to soothe her despair,
Since your swain's o'er the plain with another fair maid,
   Take my love for his, and chase away thy care,
   Who was faithless as thou, sweet maid, art fair.

The foregoing pastoral, although apparently of English extraction, is one of a numerous class of compositions, now almost extinct, in a perfect state, from the Western Shires of Scotland; these acknowledge sweet plaintive airs of their own, but now are gliding fast down into oblivion's vale, along with the chants themselves.

All the fragments of olden Song, we at present recollect any thing about (and these are not a few), along with entire pieces, which have been borne down to us by tradition, are accompanied by some characteristic air or other, peculiar to themselves, which might still be redeemed from perishing, were the snatches of song taken down, and committed to paper, as they fall from the lips of our native-taught peasantry. These reminiscences assimilate upon the mind with each other, till called up unconsciously again, when

P

a note of the one or a line of the other breaks in upon the fancy,
thereby embodying the whole anew into a Song, long unheeded,
perhaps, and half forgotten there; a bar or two is chanted; we
strain our fancy anew, to recollect the words, and soon arouse it
from this state of pristine dormancy, by gathering together all the
dismembered links of the chain, into a continuous whole. It is
difficult at times, to define the minute workings of the mind upon
paper, even upon such a trifling subject as the one we have just
now been tiring our readers with.

BEAUTY ASLEEP.

As I went out on an evening clear,
   Down by yon shady grove,
With pensive steps, I wander'd on,
   Till there I spied my love;
As she lay sleeping on the grass,
   So beautiful and fair:
Had you seen the lass, you would have sworn
   The Queen of Love was there.

The spring-flowers bent their gentle stems,
   Above the dreaming maid,
Where zephyr bade the primrose-breath,
   Diffuse where she was laid;
The small birds sang, their mates replied,
   To soothe the virgin's dream:
May the draps in life's cup, aye be as sweet
   To thee, as now they seem.

There are twelve months into the year,
    Some sad, some sweet, and gay;
But the merriest months in all the year,
    Are the months of June and May.
These are the months I'll choose my love,
    Their blythness me inspire:
Young women carry the keys of love,
    Men's hearts are still on fire.

The first and concluding stanzas of the foregoing, are here revived from an old traditional Ballad, while the intermediate verse
is original. The piece acknowledges a very pretty and characteristic air of its own, not yet, we presume, noted down.

This Ballad is another of that peculiar class of compositions,
which still lingeringly retain their hold amongst the peasantry in
the West of Scotland, a literal version of which cannot now be
" conveyed to a cleanly mind, by any language, translation, or
periphrasis whatever," and whose plot ought rather to have come
under the surveillance of the judge than of the poet. It is singular
to find such a number of our old traditional chants striking into the
same vein of perversion and gross indelicacy, without the slightest
assignable reason or necessity, while our own romantic and pastoral
country presented so many darling themes for the chaste and
sportive muse, to cull her flower, from the sweets scattered in such
profusion around her fairy footsteps.

BONNIE BEDS OF ROSES.

As I was a walking one morning in May,
The small birds were singing delightfully and gay,
Where I with my true love did often sport and play,
    Down amang the bonnie beds of roses.

My pretty brown girl, come sit on my knee,
For there's none in the world I can fancy but thee;
Nor ever will I change my old love for a new,
  So my pretty brown girl do not leave me.

My daddy and mammy they often used to say,
That I was a naughty boy, and wont to run away;
If they bid me go to work, I would sooner run to play,
  Down amang the bonnie beds of roses.

If ever I will marry, I will marry in the spring,
When small birds are singing, and summer's coming in,
By glens where rows the burnie, and wandering echoes ring,
  Down amang yon bonnie beds of roses.

As I was a walking one morning in the spring,
The winter going out, and the summer coming in,
The cuckoo sang, cuckoo, you're welcome here again!
  And I pray you stay amang the green bushes.

    The foregoing has been collated with two several copies, the one
a stall, and the other, a traditional one.   It belongs to that class of
simple pastoral chants, which have been preserved from perishing,
chiefly on account of their accompanying airs, that of the present
being among the sweetest of our old traditional melodies.

BESSY BELL AN' MARY GRAY.

O Bessy Bell an' Mary Gray,
  They were twa bonnie lassies;
They biggit a house on yon burn-brae,
  An' theekit it o'er wi' rashes:

They theekit it o'er wi' birk and brume,
 They theekit it o'er wi' heather,
Till the pest cam' frae the neib'rin town,
 An' streekit them baith thegither,

They were na' buried in Meffen kirk-yard,
 Amang the rest o' their kin;
But they were buried by Dornoch-haugh,
 On the bent before the sun:
Sing, Bessy Bell an' Mary Gray,
 They were twa bonnie lasses,
Wha' biggit a bower on yon burn-brae,
 An' theekit it o'er wi' thrashes.

The above fragment is here collated from the singing of two aged persons, one of them a native of Perthshire. It is to be regretted, that none of the intermediate stanzas of this fine old Ballad are upon record; neither Bannatyne nor Maitland, have the Ballad entered into their MSS. whilst all the information gained respecting it, is obtained from country traditions.

Elizabeth Bell is said to have been a gentleman's daughter in Perthshire, while Mary Gray belonged to the house of Lindoch. The ladies were intimate friends, and while the plague raged in Scotland, in 1666, they retired to a glen near Lindoch, to avoid the contagion, and there built for themselves a bower, where they might have remained in security, until its fury had been spent, but for the imprudence of a young gentleman, ardently attached to one of the young ladies, and who imparted to both the contagion, when they drooped and died. A large flat stone rests above their remains, pointing out to strangers the site of their interment.

PRETTY PEG OF DERBY.

A Captain of Irish Dragoons on parade,
While his regiment was stationed in Derby, O,
  Fell in love, as it is said,
  With a young blooming maid,
Though he sued in vain·to win pretty Peggy, O.

To-morrow I must leave thee, pretty Peggy, O,
Though my absence may not grieve thee, pretty Peggy, O,
  Braid up thy yellow hair,
  Ere thou tripp'st it down the stair,
And take farewell of me, thy soldier laddie, O.

Ere the dawn's reveillie sounds to march, I'm ready, O,
To make my pretty Peg a Captain's lady, O,
  Then, what would your mammy think,
  To hear the guineas clink,
And the hautboys playing before thee, O.

Must I tell you, says she, as I've told you before,
With your proffers of love, not to tease me more,
  For I never do intend,
  Ere to go to foreign land,
Or follow to the wars a soldier laddie, O.

Out spake a brother officer, the gallant De Lorn,
As he eyed the haughty maiden, with pity and scorn,
  Never mind, we'll have gallore
  Of pretty girls more,
When we've come to the town of Kilkenny, O.

But when they had come to Kilkenny, O,
Where the damsels were lovely and many, O,
    Sighing deeply, he would say,
    Though we're many miles away,
Let us pledge a health to pretty Peg of Derby, O.

Collated with a copy taken down from recitation, we never having seen the original Ballad in print. The opening stanza of this once popular piece, whose air has been adapted to songs without number, and latterly, by Moor, for his " Eveleen's Bower," is the best, which we here present to our readers in its original dress:

    O there was a regiment of Irish dragoons,
    And they were marching through Derby, O,
        The Captain fell in love
        With a young chamber-maid,
    And her *name* it was *called* pretty Peggy, O.

THE SHANNON SIDE.

'TWAS in the month of April,
   One morning by the dawn,
When violets and cowslips,
   Bestrewed every lawn,
Where Flora's flowery mantle,
   Bedeck'd the fields with pride,
I met a lovely damsel,
   Down by the Shannon side.

" Good-morrow, pretty fair one,"
   To the maiden I did say;
" Why are you up so early,
   And how far go you this way?"

With cheeks like blooming roses,
 The damsel she replied,
" I go to feed my father's sheep,
 Down by the Shannon side."

From budding elm, and branching thorn,
 Each little native sung,
But wilder thrilling melody,
 Down glen and greenwood rung;
As o'er the velvet moss we pass'd,
 Where Erin's daughters glide,
And flit along the Sylvan shores,
 And bowers on Shannon side.

We kiss'd, shook hands, and parted,
 When the bud was on the breer;
I did not come that way again,
 Till autumn sered the year,
When crossing o'er a pleasant lawn,
 By chance, my love I spied
Beside her father's bleating flock,
 Down by the Shannon side.

I never dream'd a maiden
 Could my wavering fancy win,
Till first I met this fair one,
 Then love he enter'd in,
And wreck'd my former peace of mind:
 I sought her for my bride,
Now happiness shall crown our days,
 Down by the Shannon side.

Altered from a well known old free Ballad of Irish extraction,
bearing the same title with the foregoing, while the third and fifth
stanzas are original.

ALONE BY THE LIGHT OF THE MOON.

WHEN fairies dance light on the grass,
  Wha revel a' night in a roun';
There, say will you meet me, sweet lass,
  Alone by the light of the moon.

Though sweet be the jessamine grove,
  And fragrant the roses in June,
More bland are the whispers of love,
  Breath'd forth by the light of the moon.

Where the nightingale perch'd on the thorn,
  Enchants every ear with her tune,
Rejoicing soft twilight's return,
  Let us meet by the light of the moon.

Yes! Rosa, will hie to her love,
  Through the glen by the burnie, as soon
As evening has silver'd the grove,
  Alone by the light of the moon.

Altered from the olden copy, while the last stanza is original.

THE LATE WOOER.

THE auld man he came over the lea,
  Ha, ha, ha, I'll no hae him,
    Out over the lea,
    He came to court me,
With his auld gray beard newly shaven.

My mither bade me marry the Laird,
   Ha, ha, ha, I'll no hae him;
      Sin' his wealth bears the bell,
      Ye may wed him yoursel',
With his auld gray beard newly shaven.

Wad mither and friends but let me alane,
   And tell the Laird, I'll no hae him,
      He'd forget to complain,
      Nor come o'er here again,
With his auld gray beard newly shaven.

First stanza old, rest original.

THERE WAS ANE MAY.

THERE was ane May, and she lo'ed nae men,
She biggit her bonny bower down in yon glen,
But now she cries dool! and a-well-a-day!
Come down the green gate, and come here away.

When bonny young Johnny came o'er the sea,
He said he saw naithing sae lovely as me;
He height me baith rings and mony braw things;
And were na' my heart light, I wad die.

He had a wee titty that lo'ed na me,
Because I was twice as bonny as she;
She rais'd such a pother 'twixt him and his mother,
That were na' my heart light, I wad die.

The day it was set, and the bridal to be,
The wife took a dwaum, and lay down to die:
She main'd and she grain'd out of dolour and pain,
Till he vowed he never wad see me again.

His kin was for ane of a higher degree,
Said, what had he to do with the like of me?
Albeit I was bonny, I was na for Johnny;
And were na my heart light, I wad die.

They said, I had neither cow nor cawf,
Nor dribbles of drink rins through the draff,
Nor pickles of meal rins through the mill e'e:
And were na my heart light, I wad die.

His titty she was baith wylie and slee,
She spied me as I came o'er the lee,
And then she ran in and made a loud din;
Believe your ain een, an' ye trow na me.

His bonnet stood aye fou round on his brow,
His auld ane looks aye as well as some's new;
But now he lets't wear ony gate it will hing,
And casts himself dowie upon the corn-bing.

And now he gangs dandering about the dykes,
And a' he dow do is to hund the tykes:
The live-lang night he ne'er steeks his eye,
And were na my heart light, I wad die.

Were I young for thee, as I hae been,
We shou'd hae been galloping down on yon green,
And linking it on the lily-white lee;
And wow gin I were but young for thee.

" There is no single word in modern English," says Lord Hales, in notes to his Selections from the Bannatyne MSS. " which corresponds with *dow:* that which approaches the nearest to it, is *list,* from which the adjective *listless.* The force of the word *dow,* is well expressed in the penultimate stanza of the foregoing Ballad. The lines alluded to, are in the description of one crossed in love, by an envious sister's machination, and a peevish mother's fro-wardness:"

And now he gangs *dandering* about the dykes,
And all he *dow* do is to *hund the tykes.*"

" The whole," continues his Lordship, " is executed with equal truth and strength of colouring."   This Ballad is the composition of Lady Grissel Baillie, daughter of Patrick, the first Earl of Marchmont, and wife of George Baillie of Jarviswood, whose widow she died in 1746.

PRESTWICK DRUM.

Air—AITKEN DRUM.

AT gloamin' gray, the close o' day,
    When saftly sinks the village hum,
Nor far nor near ought meets the ear,
    But aiblins Prestwick drum.
Nae bluidy battle it betides,
Nor sack, nor siege, nor ought besides,
Twa gude sheep-skins, wi' oaken sides,
    An' leather lugs aroun'.

In days o' yore, when to our shore,
    For aid the gallant Bruce did come,
His lieges leal, did tak' the fiel',
    An' march'd to Prestwick drum.
Gude service aften is forgot,
An' favour won by crafty plot,
An' sik, alas! has been the lot
    O' Prestwick's ancient drum.

" The original charter of Prestwick is now lost, but is referred
to, in the renewed grant by James VI. of Scotland. Bruce having
at first been unsuccessful, after passing some time in exile, re-
appeared in Arran, and crossing the Frith, landed on Prestwick
shore, where the inhabitants joined his standard in considerable
force; for which service, the king was pleased to erect their town
into a barony, with a jurisdiction extending from the Water of
Ayr to the Water of Irvine."

THE BAILLIE'S DAUGHTER OF BONNY DUNDEE.

Oh, have I burned, or have I slain,
    Or have I done ought of injury!
I've slighted the lass I may ne'er see again,
    The Baillie's daughter of bonny Dundee.

Bonny Dundee, and bonny Dundas,
    Where shall I meet sae comely a lass!
Open your ports and let me gang free,
    I maunna stay langer in bonny Dundee!

It is barely necessary to mention here, that the two concluding lines of the above lively fragment, are those sung by
Rob Roy, towards the finale of his midnight interview with
Baillie Nicol Jarvie, in the Tolbooth of Glasgow. See the
historical novel of " Rob Roy."

WILL YE GO TO ALDAVALLOCH.

IMITATED FROM THE GAELIC.

Will ye go to Aldavalloch?
Will ye go to Aldavalloch?
Sweet the mellow mavis sings,
Amang the braes of Aldavalloch.

There, beneath the spreading boughs,
  Amang the woods of green Glenfalloch,
Softly murmuring as it flows,
  Winds the pure stream of Aldavalloch.

The first golden smile of morn,
  And the last beam that evening sheddeth,
Baith that echoing vale adorn—
  That brightly glows, this mildly fadeth.

Short is there hoar winter's stay,
  When spring returns like Hebe blooming—
Hand in hand with rosy May,
  With balmy breath the air perfuming.

But there's a flower, a fairer flower
  Than ever grew in green Glenfalloch,
The blithesome maiden I adore,
  Young blooming May of Aldavalloch.

Let me but pu' this opening rose,
    And fondly press it to my bosom;
I ask no other flower that blows,
    Be mine this modest little blossom.

"The lady who favoured the public with the well-known Song called 'Roy's Wife,' says a writer in the Literary Chronicle, forgot to mention the obligation she lay under to the original, of which the above is a close imitation, and, in some instances, a literal translation. This beautiful air is at least a hundred and twenty years old, for I learned it twenty-eight years ago, from a Mrs. M'Hardy, who was then in the hundred and sixth year of her age, and who said, that when a little girl, she had learned it of her mother; whereas, the Scottish words to the same tune have not been known half that time. Indeed, the greater part of the old Scottish melodies may be traced back to the Gaelic bards: 'The ewie wi' the crooked horn,' 'The rock and the wee pickle tow,' &c. are of Gaelic original, and have been known in the Highlands from time immemorial. As I am now upon this subject, I cannot help mentioning, that the last stanza of 'Roy's Wife' has been rendered downright nonsense, by the creation of the uncouth term Walloch, in order to rhyme with the proper name, Aldavalloch. New words are daily invented, to designate things not already adequately described, but no such dance as 'The Highland Walloch' ever did exist, though any one but a Highlander, on reading the stanza in question, would be led to suppose the reverse."

THE ADIEU.

THE boatmen shout, "'tis time to part,
    No longer can we stay;"
'Twas thus Maimuna taught my heart,
    How much a glance could say.

With trembling steps to me she came;
    "Farewell," she would have cried!
But ere her lips the word could frame,
    In half-form'd sounds it died.

Then kneeling down with looks of love,
    Her arms she round me flung;
And as the gale hangs on the grove,
    Upon my breast she hung.

My willing arms embraced the maid,
    My heart with raptures beat;
While she but wept the more, and said,
    "Would we had never met."

Abou Mohammed, a celebrated musician of Bagdad, says Professor Carlyle in his Selections from Arabian Poetry, 1810, being desired to produce a specimen of his abilities before the Khaliph Wathek, A. Hejræ 227, sung the foregoing, and such were its effects upon the Khaliph, that he immediately testified his approbation of the performance, by throwing his own robe over the poet's shoulders, and ordering him to receive a present of one hundred thousand dirhams.

Twenty-two and a half dirhams, according to our authority, the Hindostan Dictionary, being about equal to nine shillings sterling, any gentle poet of calculation may, at his leisure, sum up the copy-right price of this eminently beautiful Eastern production.

MATILDA'S DREAM.

NIGHT closed around: in gusts the hail
    Beat furious down the rocky steep:
Matilda's ruddy cheek grew pale,
    As the blast yell'd round in angry sweep.

The thunders roll'd above the wood,
　The red-stream'd lightnings play'd around;
Near a lone blasted oak she stood,
　Where the pale glow-worms lit the ground.

Where can I rest my wearied form,
　In frantic mood the lady cried,
Or shield my baby from the storm?
　And such a storm!—she wept and sigh'd.

Where loud waves round the dark clifts beat,
　A flickering gleam of light she spied;
Cold shivering through the driving sleet,
　O'er the sharp flinty rocks she hied.

The scorched heath, and the feathery brake,
　Hung withering o'er the dingle's side,
As lorn she wander'd by the lake,
　With the struggling moonbeams for her guide:

Unseemly weeds of varied hue,
　Grew round the cavern tall and rank;
Here, drop-wort—there, the monk's hood blue,
　Tangled the dark lake's hoary bank.

In sooth, this was as wild a scene,
　As mortal eye had ere survey'd;
Or fancy dream'd could ere have been,
　Found on the world, where'er we stray'd.

Unearthly sounds thrill'd on the ear,
 Which grew not with the passing blast;
But rose from 'neath the night-shade drear,
 Scaring the gray-owl screaming past.

Hush, baby! though the warring wind
 Ring louder its rude lullaby,
It cannot be to thee unkind,
 Nor harm my darling should he cry.

Here lay thee down, this mossy bed
 Is soft and warm; calm be thy sleep,
Sound thy repose, as round thy head
 I strew the fern, and vigil keep.

Within the cavern's deep recess,
 She heard the plaintive voice of woe;
It's wail was one of deep distress,
 Dying away in accents slow.

A well-known voice assails her ear;—
 My Henry's! hark! another groan,
The helping hand of heaven be near,
 O shield him, leave him not alone!

The struggle's o'er, the echoes die,
 That rose within the rock-bound cave,
Save where a deep convulsive sigh,
 Half-drown'd within the tempest's rave,

Appeal'd for mercy to the foe,
　Who raised above the wounded man
His sword, and aim'd a deadly blow,
　While shrieking wild, Matilda ran,

Like maniac frenzied to despair,
　And grasp'd the ruffian's pointed steel;
O spare his life! my Henry spare!
　For my soul's dear love compassion feel.

O ruffian! soothe thy ill-timed rage,
　He never harm'd thee: could'st thou know
His worth as I do, thou'dst assuage
　Thy fell revenge, and pity show.

The frowning villain's eye grew bright,
　He seiz'd Matilda's trembling hand:
If fiend from stygian shades of night
　Can feign to smile, and whisper bland,

That smile's unearthly; for his rung
　Wild aspirations through the hall;
While she on the fainting victim clung—
　Life's ebbing wave, essay'd to recall.

Wild thoughts now flit across her mind,
　Despair chased every hope away;
Nor left one sunny ray behind,
　To soothe the chillings of dismay.

The ruffian frown'd, and stood aghast,
  But not appall'd—then rudely rais'd
The trembling fair one, while he cast
  A blighting look around, then gazed

On this drooping flower, whose slender form,
  Bent like a lily to the blast,
Too gentle for the warring storm,
  And scenes like these which round her pass'd.

Her head grew giddy, bodings wild
  Throbb'd quickly through her maddening brain;
My husband!—then she cried, my child!
  In heaven alone our hopes remain.

While lashing waves their fury spent,
  Around the cave in angry foam;
She mark'd the ruffian's dire intent,
  To ingulf her in a watery tomb.

Who open'd the storm-beat grating wide,
  Deep rushing waters round them throng;
He flung her on the foamy tide,
  Howling the craggy rocks among.

She started—shriek'd—'twas but a dream!
  In slumbers light her Henry slept;
Her baby smiled—the morning's beam
  Shone bright on all: for joy she wept.

                                        EDITOR.

NURSERY CHANT.

In the gowany meadow there grows a grove,
    Fine flowers in the valley;
And a bonny bird sings frae the boughs above,
    Where the rose waves o'er the lily.

His lightsome trillings of glee were heard,
    Fine flowers in the valley;
By the tod beeking lown in the greeny sward,
    Where the rose nods o'er the lily.

The bird lap down on the bloomy breer,
    Fine flowers in the valley;
Nor thought tod-lowrie lay sae near,
    Where the rose bent o'er the lily.

Whase heart's blood sprents thy snaw-white bloom,
    Quo' the red rose to the lily?
Oh! the bird's that sang frae the boughs, perfume
    Where thy blush-leaves strew the valley.

                      EDITOR.

LOGIE O' BUCHAN.

O Logie o' Buchan, O Logie the laird,
They've ta'en awa Jamie, that delved in the yard,
Wha play'd on the pipe, wi' the viol sae sma';
They've ta'en awa Jamie, the flower o' them a'.

He said, think na lang, lassie, though I gang awa;
He said, think na lang, lassie, though I gang awa;
For simmer is coming, cauld winter's awa,
And I'll come and see thee in spite o' them a.'

Sandy has ousen, has gear, and has kye;
A house and a hadden, and siller forbye:
But I'd tak my ain lad, wi' his staff in his hand,
Before I'd hae him, wi' his houses and land.

My daddie looks sulky, my minnie looks sour,
They frown upon Jamie because he is poor:
Though I lo'e them as weel as a daughter should do,
They're nae hauf sae dear to me, Jamie, as you.

I sit on my creepie, I spin at my wheel,
And think on the laddie that lo'ed me sae weel;
He had but ae saxpence, he brak it in twa,
And gi'ed me the hauf o't when he gade awa.

Then haste ye back, Jamie, and bide na awa,
Then haste ye back, Jamie, and bide na awa;
The simmer is coming, cauld winter's awa,
And ye'll come and see me in spite o' them a'.

The above song, upon the authority of Mr. Buchan of Peterhead, is the composition of Mr. George Halket, and was written by him while he was a Schoolmaster at Rathen, Aberdeenshire, about the year 1736. His poetry was chiefly Jacobitical, and long remained familiar amongst the peasantry in that quarter of the country: one of the best known of these, at the present day, is "Wherry, Whigs awa man." In 1746, Mr. Halket wrote a dialogue betwixt George II. and the Devil," which falling into the Duke of Cumberland's hands, while on his march to Culloden, he offered one hundred pounds reward for the person or the head of its author. Mr. Halket died in the year 1756.

The Logie here mentioned, is in one of the adjoining parishes (Crimond), where Mr. Halket then resided; and the hero of the piece, was a James Robertson, gardener at the place of Logie. The original Ballad, commences thus:

> O woe to Kinmundy, Kinmundy the Laird,
> Wha's tane awa Jamie, that delved i' the yard,
> Wha play'd on the pipe, an' the viol sae sma',
> Kinmundy's ta'en Jamie, the flower o' them a.'

DE'IL TAK THE WARS.

De'il tak the wars that hurried Billy from me,
    Who to love me just had sworn;
They made him captain, sure, to undo me!
    Woe's me! he'll ne'er return.
A thousand loons abroad will fight him,
    He from thousands ne'er will run:
Day and night I did invite him,
    To stay at home from sword and gun.
        I used alluring graces,
        With many kind embraces,
Now sighing, then crying, tears dropping fall;
        And had he my soft arms
        Preferr'd to war's alarms,
By love grown mad, without the help of God,
    I fear in my fit I had granted all.

I washed and patched to make me look provoking,
  Snares that they told me would catch the men;
And on my head a huge commode sat poking,
  Which made me show as tall again:
For a new gown, too, I paid muckle money,
  Which with golden flowers did shine;
My love well might think me gay and bonny,
  No Scots lass was e'er so fine.

      My petticoat I spotted,
      Fringe, too, with thread I knotted,
Lace shoes, and silk hose garter'd full o'er knee;
      But, oh! the fatal thought,
      To Billy these are nought;
Who rode to towns, and rifled with dragoons,
  When he, silly loon, might have married me.

In one of Walsh the London Music-seller's early publications, about the year 1700, entitled, " A Collection of the Choicest Songs and Dialogues, composed by the most eminent masters of the age," &c. the foregoing Song occurs, and is thus introduced upon the reader's notice: " De'il tak the wars," a Song, in ' A Wife for any Man,' the words by Mr. Thomas Durffey, set to music by Mr. Charles Powell, sung by Mrs. Cross, and exactly engraved by Mr. Thomas Cross." &c. In turning over an old MS. collection of Scottish airs, in our possession, we find one of them entitled, " Foul fa' the wars," which inclines us to think, that some earlier Song than the foregoing, perhaps of Scottish extraction, has been picked up by D'Urfey, and altered to what we now find it.

Tom D'Urfey (as he usually is styled) was a facetious English writer, born, according to one authority, in France, and by another in Exeter. He was author of several Comedies, besides numerous Poems and Songs, published betwixt 1672 and 1721. A large collection of which, in 1719, were printed in 6 volumes, 12mo. under the title of " Wit and Mirth, or Pills to Purge Melancholy." He died in the year 1723.

TO THE EVENING STAR.

WHEN from the blue sky traces of the day-light
Fade, and the night-winds sigh from the ocean,
Then, on thy watch-tower, beautiful thou shinest,
   Star of the evening!

Homewards weary man plods from his labour;
From the dim vale comes the low of the oxen;
Still are the woods, and the wings of the small birds
   Folded in slumber.

Thou art the lover's star, thou to his fond heart
Ecstacy bequeathest; for, beneath thy soft ray,
Underneath the green trees, down by the river, he
   Waits for his fair one.

Thou to the sad heart beacon art of solace,
Kindly the mourner turns his gaze towards thee,
Past joys awakening, thou bidst him be of comfort,
   Smiling in silence.

Star of the mariner! when the dreary ocean
Welters around him, and the breeze is moaning,
Fondly he dreams that thy bright eye is dwelling
   On his home afar off—

On the dear cottage, where sit by the warm hearth,
Thinking of the absent, his wife and his dear babes,
In his ear sounding, the hum of their voices
   Steals like a zephyr.

Farewell, thou bright Star! when woe and anguish
Hung on my heart with a heavy and sad load,
When not a face on the changed earth was friendly,
   Changeless didst thou smile.

Soon shall the day come, soon shall the night flee,
Thou dost usher in darkness and day-light;
Glitter'st through the storm, and 'mid the blaze of morning,
   Meltest in glory.

Thus through this dark earth holds on the good man,
Misfortune and malice tarnish not his glory;
Soon the goal is won, and the star of his being
   Mingles with heaven.

       ANON.

THE DREAM.

DISTRACTED with anguish, and weary in mind,
 I threw myself myself down at the close of the night;
Sleep deign'd in compassion, my eyelids to bind,
And for once, did an angel of mercy prove kind,
 For he sent me a dream of delight.

I dream'd that the ardour of love made me bold,
 And hasten'd my footsteps to Anne again;
I repeated the vows I had utter'd of old;
That my tongue was ne'er false, and my heart never cold;
 And implored her to chase away sorrow and pain.

With transport I saw when my angel did hear,
 That her bosom to kindness and pity was true:
She approved my attachment, and found it sincere;
She soothed the poor soul that held her so dear;
 And bade him bid sorrow and sighing adieu.

I wept with delight,—she alone had the art,
 From the wild war of passions my bosom to save;
I bless'd the fair beam that spoke peace to my heart,
And swore in my rapture, we never should part,
 But live in one mansion,—repose in one grave!

But ah! cruel fancy, how illusive thy pleasure,
 In the morning I woke, but to sorrow again;
I'll curse the day-light, that robed me of my treasure,
I'll give my sad soul to despair without measure,
 I'll wear out my sad life, in sorrow and pain.

The foregoing rhapsody, taken down from the recitation of a
Lady, is ascribed to the celebrated Rev. Dr. C*******, and is
said to have been written by him, while a student at college.

THE KING'S LEA-MERE.

THE damsel stood to watch the fight,
 By the banks of the King's Lea-Mere;
And they brought to her feet her own true knight,
 Sore wounded, on a bier.

She knelt by him, his wounds to bind,
　　She wash'd them with many a tear;
And shouts rose fast upon the wind,
　　Which told that the foe was near.

" O let not," he said, " while yet I live,
　　The cruel foe me take;
But with thy sweet lips, a last kiss give,
　　And cast me in the lake."

Around his neck, she wound her arms,
　　And she kiss'd his lips so pale;
And evermore the war's alarms,
　　Came louder up the vale.

She drew him to the lake's steep side,
　　Where the red heath fringed the shore;
She plung'd with him beneath the tide,
　　And they were seen no more.

Their true blood mingled in King's Lea-Mere,
　　That to mingle on earth were fain;
And the trout that swims in that crystal clear,
　　Is tinged with the crimson stain.

　　　From the historical Novel of " Maid Marian."

FROM SCHILLER'S " WILHELM TELL."
Air.—" THE RANZ DES VACHES."

THE lake's dimpled waters to bathing invite;
On its shore sleeps a youth lapp'd in dreams of delight,
Whilst he hears a soft murmur like flutes in the air,
Like voices of angels in Paradise fair;

But when he awakes from his soothing repose,
High over his bosom the cool water flows,
And from under the billow, resounds, thou art mine!
I lure the fond shepherd where suns never shine.

Farewell, sunny fields, where my cattle have fed,
The herdsman departs when the summer has fled;
We haste to the vale, we return to the mountain,
Where cuckoos call gaily, and birds warble sweet,
When May, genial May, shall dissolve the charm'd fountain,
And earth yield new flowers to the wanderer's feet;
Farewell sunny fields, where my cattle have fed,
The herdsman departs when the summer has fled.

The lofty crags thunder, and totters the way;
Along with the hunter, must follow his prey,
Undaunted, he ventures o'er heap'd ice and snow,
Where spring is a stranger, where flowers never blow;
Underneath mountain mists, spread a sea without shore,
And the cities of men, are distinguish'd no more,
Only through cloudy openings, the world can he spy,
Where under their waters, the green meadows lie.

In the *Zeitschwingen*, there is an article entitled " Eight Days in Weimar and Jena," which contains the following passage:— " The evening sun found me on Schiller's grave, which was pointed out to me by the sexton. In the park of Weimar, a dog was buried, and the place where it lies, is marked by a stone with an inscription;—but the graves of Herder and Schiller are not even honoured with their immortal names. Thus have I satisfied my curiosity, and seen Weimar, and seen that there was not much to see. The epoch when Wieland, Herder, Goethe, and Schiller lived here, may indeed have been a different one; but it was not the right one, as it has gone by without leaving a trace behind."

Frederic Schiller, M. D. Professor of Philosophy at Jena, was born at Morbach, in Wurtemburgh, 1759, died 1805.

THE TANE-AWAY.

THE summer sun was sinking
  With a mild light calm and mellow,
It shone on my little boy's bonny cheeks,
  And his loose locks of yellow.

The robin was singing sweetly,
  And his song was sad and tender;
And my little boy's eyes, while he heard the song,
  Smiled with a sweet soft splendour.

My little boy lay on my bosom,
  While his soul the song was quaffing,
The joy of his soul had tinged his cheek,
  ·And his heart and his eye were laughing.

I sat alone in my cottage,
  The midnight needle plying;
I feared for my child, for the rush's light
  In the socket now was dying.

There came a hand to my lonely latch,
  Like the wind at midnight moaning;
I knelt to pray, but rose again,
  For I heard my little boy groaning.

I cross'd my brow, and I cross'd my breast,
  But that night my child departed;
They left a weakling in his stead,
  And I am broken-hearted.

Oh! it cannot be my own sweet boy,
  For his eyes are dim and hollow,
My little boy is gone to God,
  And his mother soon will follow.

The dirge for the dead will be sung for me,
  And the mass be chanted meetly;
And I will sleep with my little boy,
  In the moonlight churchyard sweetly.

" The woman, in whose character these lines are written, sup-
poses her child stolen by a fairy.   I need not mention how pre-
valent the superstition is in Ireland, which attributes most instances
of sudden death to the agency of these spirits."—Translated from
the German, by John Anster, Esq.

THE ORPHAN MAID.

NOVEMBER's hail-cloud drifts away,
  November's sun-beam wan
Looks coldly on the castle gray,
  When forth comes Lady Anne.

The orphan by the oak was set,
  Her arms, her feet were bare,
The hail-drops had not melted yet,
  Amid her raven hair.

" And, dame," she said, " by all the ties
  That child and mother know,
Aid one who never knew these joys,
  Relieve an orphan's woe."

The lady said, " An orphan's state
   Is hard and sad to bear;
Yet worse the widow'd mother's fate,
   Who mourns both lord and heir.

" Twelve times the rolling year has sped,
   Since, while from vengeance wild
Of fierce Strathallan's chief I fled,
   Forth's eddies whelmed my child."

" Twelve times the year its course has born,"
   The wandering maid replied,
" Since fishers on St. Bridget's morn
   Drew nets on Campsie side.

" St. Bridget sent no scaly spoil—
   An infant, well nigh dead,
They saved, and rear'd in want and toil,
   To beg from you her bread."

That orphan maid the lady kiss'd,—
   " My husband's looks you bear;
Saint Bridget and her morn be bless'd!
   You are his widow's heir."

They've robed that maid, so poor and pale,
   In silk and sandals rare;
And pearls, for drops of frozen hail,
   Are glistening in her hair.

                           ANON.

THE BITTER PARTING.

AIR.—" GRAMACHREE."

ADIEU, my false inconstant love,
 My conflict now is o'er,
And peace pervades that stormy breast,
 Where passions raged before;
No tenderness my eye illumes,
 Nor heaves my feverish breath,
My heart with anguish worn, assumes
 A stillness, calm as death.

There was a time, when in my breast,
 A mutual flame did burn,
Thou wouldst my kiss unshrinking meet,
 My ardent press return;
But scenes of tender heart-felt love,
 Now fade upon my view,
And no remembrance memory gives,
 Save, thou wert aught but true.

        W. M.

THE SAILOR BOY.

I loved by the bonny river Clyde,
 To wander the lonely shore;
To hear the Sailor's song in the breeze,
 And the wild wave's dashing roar.

There Willy first told me his tale of love,
 And my fond heart beat with joy;
Oh! nought on earth was so sweet to my ear,
 As the voice of my Sailor boy.

He told me of far, far distant lands,
 And of dangers he braved on the main,
And said he would face them a thousand times o'er,
 For the sake of his lovely Jane.

But Willy went to sea; and my heart
 No more can throb with joy;
For the hand of death, in a distant land,
 Has been laid on my Sailor boy.

And now, by the shores of bonny Clyde,
 The Sailor's song and the wave,
Makes my poor heart chill, for they tell of him
 That's laid in the cold, cold grave.

          H.

THE MENDICANT.

I have no home of refuge here,
 In poverty, without a friend,
To mix with mine one kindly tear—
 Alone, I through the world bend
With Cæsar here, my playful pet,
My little all, and my flageolet.

And with its light heart-stirring sound,
   I strive to please the village boys;
Even Cæsar he will dance around,
   And, when I pipe, with them rejoice;
While by the fire, on winter's eve,
I sit, and pleasing stories weave.

And am I poor, or wretched then,
   Who in the beams of mercy live?
I've learn'd to spurn the joys of men,
   And prize a boon they cannot give—
A peace within, that cheers my way—
A boon that none can take away.

Heaven knows that I have many cares,
   Submissive, let me bow to fate;
My fortune brings me weighty fears,
   My Cæsar and my flageolet!
But when my wanderings here are past,
I'll get a home in heaven at last.

J. B. Thomson.

IT IS DAY.

It is day, it is day,
   Lovely maid, come away,
Let us welcome the blush of the dawn;
   The bird upon the tree,
   He is singing merrily,
And the shepherd whistles blythe o'er the lawn;
All nature is awake, and every thing is gay,
   For now it is day, it is day.

It is day, it is day,
    Wreathy shadows flee away,
Rosy health is on the wings of the gale,
        Even sorrow's griefs are fled,
        And pale sickness leaves her bed,
To gather fresh flowers in the vale,
Each sense breathes delight, each pulse is in play,
        For O it is day, it is day.

It is day, it is day,
    Lovely Peggy, come away,   `
Let us brush the fresh dews from the green,
        Each fresh little flower,
        Peeping forth from beauty's bower,
Smiles around on the fairy-colour'd scene;   [spray,
Young summer breathes around, and the linnet from his
Tells the glens and the woods, it is day.

                            J. B. THOMSON.

THE FLOWER OF ERNE.

PLEASANT were the hours by Erne's stream a-wandering,
    But sad was the parting adieu,   [presence,
Bade us steal from sweet scenes, so endear'd by thy
    Where each word and look show'd thee true.

How oft in the rapture of love's joyous moments,
    To range through yon wood we were used,
And how bless'd with my love, in yon wild rosy bower,
    On her sweet winning features I've mused.

Why droops the lily fair, and each gay woodland flower,
 And why croaks the hoarse raven along,
And why, O gentle Erne, far along thy Sylvan shore,
 Hush the small birds their evening song?

But hark! yon doleful knell, and see yon sable band,
 Oh! they bear my dear Helen away;
And now her purer soul breathes its own etherial air,
 In the clime of the aye cloudless day.

Cease, then, my fond heart, no more must thou ponder,
 On scenes by remembrance held dear,
For past are all your charms, even love's gay illusions,
 That once wont this bosom to cheer.

PETER TAIT.

GUDE NIGHT AN' JOY BE WI' YOU A'.

THE year is wearin' to the wane,
 An' day is fading west awa',
Loud raves the torrent an' the rain,
 An' dark the cloud comes down the shaw.
But let the tempest tout an' blaw,
 Upon his loudest winter born,
Gude night an' joy be wi' you a',
 We'll maybe meet again the morn.

S

O we hae wander'd far an' wide,
    O'er Scotia's land of firth an' fell;
An' mony a simple flower we've cull'd,
    An' twined them wi' the heather-bell:
We've ranged the dingle an' the dell,
    The hamlet, an' the baron's ha',
Now let us tak' a kind farewell,
    Gude night an' joy be wi' you a'.

Ye hae been kind as I was keen,
    And follow'd where I led the way,
Till ilka poet's lore we've seen,
    Of this an' mony a former day:
If e'er I led your steps astray,
    Forgi'e your minstrel ance for a',
A tear fa's wi' his partin' lay,
    Gude night an' joy be wi' you a'.

HOGG.

SECTION IV.

POEMS BY THE EDITOR.

POEMS BY THE EDITOR.

MY NATIVE GLEN.

En unquam patrios, longo post tempore fines,
Post aliquot mea regna videns, mirabor aristas?
VIRGIL.

MELLOW thy notes, fond bird! thy small shrill voice,
　Without a pause since morn, has rung along
The echoing glen;—the listening fawns rejoice,
　Around me, at thy wild intrusive song.

My footsteps linger where thy melody
　Floats soft around the gay liburnum's shade;
Whose yellow drooping garlands round the tree,
　Diffuse fresh odours where thy songs pervade,

And die away in echoes;—mazing round
　The waving forest boughs of glossiest green,
In smiling summer's verdure; bless'd the sound,
　That wakes delight, and gladdens all the scene!

Here from the burning rays of noontide's sun,
  Beneath the tangling hazel boughs again,
I sit me down, where the rippling waters run,
  In mournful cadence past me throughout the glen.

Then eddying round yon woodbine-faced defile,
  A beaming mirror leaps the white cascade,
Bright glancing to the sunshine's radiant smile,
  Showering its spray around the coppiced glade,

Where hoary wild-thyme cushions o'er the rocks,
  'Tis fair to view in such a lonely scene,
The stately tod-flax wave her yellow locks,   .
  And starry-saxifrage around the green.

And sun-dew, with the whortle-berry's bell;
  Like hectic maid, when love lights up her smile;
And laughing eye-bright, with the asphodel,
  And rose-bay-willow, on the rock's defile;

And dusky crane's-bill blushing by her side,
  And gaudy fox-glove's drooping purple bells,
And nodding hyacinth, the wild wood's pride,
  And birds-eye-primrose, beauty of the dells.

The clustering hawthorn, fondling o'er the rose,
  Shading the modest violet in its turn;
While the bright champion all her beauty shows,
  Above the sparkling bosom of the burn.

Unnumber'd flowers bestrewn by nature's hand,
 In fair luxuriance bud and bloom around;
While fancy reigns, and smiles upon the land,
 Above, and round this consecrated ground.

My native glen! from you, when far away,
 My dreams will still inhale your fresh perfume,
Where through the woodruff's fragrancy I stray,
 Or linger round the yellow banks of broom.

At morn, when all around is hush'd in sleep,
 Ere the early sun dispels the morning dews,
I leave the haunts of men in silence deep,
 Within your dark and leafy dells to muse;

Or wander o'er the bushy mountain's brow,
 Around the amphitheatre of woods;
Sombering the landscape in the vale below,
 Where brawling comes the voice of rushing floods

Unseen, while yet the wreathing mists impend,
 Curling above the lonesome green wood's reign;
While far below the foaming streams descend,
 Leaping from rock to lin, to reach the plain.

'Tis sweet in such a lovely wilderness,
 Ere sleeping flowers their dewy breasts unfold
To the morning's sun, the tufted lawn to press,
 And hear the matin song ring through the wold.

In scenes like these, remote from human bield,
    Oh could I pass the vale of life alone,
In peace with th' calm, a rural life might yield,
    And hail yon moss-crown'd cavern as my own.

Fond recollections! glens, and woods, and all
    Ye kindred ties that long and firm have been
Twining around this heart, when I recall
    Your dear remembrance, like a morning's dream.

On some far distant day, when seas between
    Us lie; Time's signet, while the warm tears glow,
Shall ne'er efface you, nor this smiling scene,
    Where all my hopes concentrate, ebb, and flow.

Mellow thy notes, sweet bird! the dingle rings
    Thy warblings louder, wouldst thou wert at rest,
And roosting on the spray: Each note thou sings,
    Thrills sadness through this throbbing fever'd breast.

VERNAL FLOWERS.

THE yellow Aconite from winter's urn,
    With many an early spring-flower in her train,
Starring the landscape, welcome spring's return,
    Awakening vegetation o'er the plain:

From glen to grove, each small bird's voice again
Rings music on the breeze—now the pleas'd eye
   Can watch the vernal flower through its short reign,
Whether its virgin bud conceal'd may lie
   'Mong wither'd leaves, or 'neath the budding thorn.
Or dips its crimson cups in the pure stream,
   Watering its new-born blossoms, while the morn
Smiles down the primrosed valley; every gleam
   Of sunshine wakens up new flowers to blow,
   So late enshrined in beds of virgin snow.

THE WIND-FLOWER.

I watch'd the Wind-Flower, as she, leaf by leaf,
   Unfolded to the breath of April's air;
Her pale and vermil petals, streak'd like grief
   On the young face of beauty, when despair
Or premature decay has seiz'd upon
   Her angel frame, and droop'd her in her prime.
The flower expanded as the sunbeams shone
   Around the smiling glade.   No fairer clime
Than this needs ere be sigh'd for, where the ground
   Is studded o'er with Wind-Flower; fleeting blooms!
To-morrow ye are gone, and no more found,
   Till spring again the wood and lawn perfumes.
     Fair emblem of my Laura's hectic bloom,
    Loved and adored, then entered in the tomb.

WRITTEN AT SEA.

IT is pleasant to gaze on the deep blue sky,
When the fair moonbeams on the waters lie,
   And the night breeze swells our sail;
When all is sea, the eye can explore,
As the bark steers for my native shore,
   With a light and steady gale.

How lovely then on the calm green sea,
To mark the fish on our starboard and lea,
   In countless shoals around,
Like a molten lake of paler gold
All sparkling bright, whose bars infold
   Our bark as on fairy ground.

As our prow glides through, we wondering gaze
On the far spread phosphorescent blaze,
   While from each curling wave,
Bright bars of gold spring up, then glide
In liquid fire down the living tide,
   The glancing brine to lave.

We near'd the shore, when the dawning morn
Illumin'd the waves, and the spell was gone;
   But never from this breast
Shall a sight so glorious and sublime,
Ere be effaced, in whatever clime
   My pilgrim'd footsteps rest.

WRITTEN AT THE CLOSE OF THE COLD SPRING, 1827.

> As yet the trembling year is unconfirm'd,
> And winter oft at eve resumes the breeze,
> Chills the pale morn, and bids his driving sleets
> Deform the day delightless.—THOMSON.

'TIS April! yet the snow-storm hovers round,
   To blight and scare thee in thy growth—sweet flower,
The flakes fall fast around thee, while the ground
   Crisps to my tread—all yield to winter's power

But thee, and the young snow-drop; left at will
   To bloom or perish in the wilds ye love,
By the hoar-drooping hawthorn 'neath the hill,
   First in pale Flora's train by yonder grove.

What poet with a scene so drear, forlorn,
   Would mantle spring, in smiling robes of green!
For see her shivering in the chills of morn,
   Where panzied tufts, and primrose beds have been

And should be blooming now, where snow-clad bowers
   Shrine April in the wilderness around,
Of fair and spotless purity, where flowers
   Shrink from the clear cold air within the ground,

And nestle their young buds in the wither'd leaves,
   Strewn by Pomona when she fled these dells:
Yet see, braving the blast, whose bosom heaves,
   Fronting the storm, whose embryo beauty swells,

And bursts its cerement; alternate spread
    Thy yellow petals smiling to the morn,
Bright gaudy golden cup! the lark o'erhead
    Will greet thee, soon as soft winds lax the storm.

Bloom on, sweet flowers; you're shelter'd in the grove,
    While all around the devious woodland shore,
Where Kelvin murmurs onward as I rove,
    Is shingled with the rime-frost spreading hoar.

As muffled in my cloak I climb the hill,
    And lean upon yon rock—the vale below,
Where winter lords, around sleeps peaceful still,
    'Mong leafless underwoods, and wreaths of snow.

How bleak appears the wide extending plain,
    To where yon dark pines throw their gloom around:
No speck of green gladdens the dreary scene,
    No wild bird warbles forth a joyous sound.

The cold east wind blows bleak o'er hill and lawn,
    Blighting the opening bud, while in his train,
Disease, with flurrying pace, from eve till dawn,
    Stalks ghastly o'er the pestilence-tainted plain.

Your rigours cannot last;—the rudest gush,
    Of passion rankling in the human breast,
Lords but its day, then settles down to blush,
    At its own futile weakness,—though oppress'd

And sear'd in April's bosom, soon will May
    Relieve her elder sister, now forlorn,
Rain her warm tears, and thaw the frosts away
    From her wan flowerless forehead.   May! thy morn

Is usher'd in by all, with odorous breaths,
    Cradled in April's lap—so poets sing,
Who strew thy path in smiles, and flowery wreaths:
    For once, distrust the tidings which they bring.

HORACE, Lib. I. Ode IX.—TO THALIARCHUS.

      Vides, ut alta, stet nive candidum
      Soracte.

BLEAK Soracte meets my sight,
Clothed in a robe of virgin white;
The olives in the vale below,
Groan beneath a load of snow,
While bound in strongest bands of frost,
The currents of the streams are lost,
One solid sheet of ice spreads o'er,
Fair Tyber's banks from shore to shore.

Dispel the cold, the friendly blaze,
To warm and cheer your poet, raise;
With wood the blazing ingle crown,
Till every object shine around.

         T

From Sabine cask thy nectar pour,
To beguile the weary hour,
Cause the sparkling goblets shine,
With four years old Falernian wine.

The cares of life, the pangs of love,
Leave them to the gods above,
Who calm the storm, and still the breeze,
Contending with the stormy seas,
When the dark cypress groves are still,
And the old beeches 'neath the hill.

What cares sit on to-morrow's brow,
Leave off to seek the sequel now;
What length of days to thee are given,
Contented wait the will of heaven.

Fond youth, disdain not love's advances,
When proffer'd thee, nor yet the dances,
Till crabbed age above thee hover,
'And thy hey-days of youth are over.

Now Campus Martius, and the streets
Of ancient Rome (where each whisper meets
The ear, when evening shadows lower),
Are sought again at the appointed hour;
And the coy maid's light-hearted smile,
Her feign'd retreats too soon beguile.—
On her arms the bracelets feebly linger,
And the ring on her gently resisting finger.

ANACREON.—Ode V.

TO THE ROSE.

Το ροδον το των ερωτων.

COME let us mingle with the purpling vine,
　The rose of love, the gay-leaf'd blushing rose;
Roses around our temples let us twine,
While laughing merrily, we quaff the wine,
　Rich in rose odours till our bosom glows.

O rose, with damask bosom! fairest flower!
　Delightful to the gods!—of teeming spring,
Thou art the cherish'd nursling!—every bower,
　Balm'd by thy breath, ten thousand odours bring.

Round his fair flowing locks, see Venus' child,
　Wreathes roses, whilst the mazy dance is led,
Through the bright rosary by the urchin wild,
　And comely graces—heaven is in their tread.

Crown me, great Bacchus, that my willing lyre,
　May hymn aloud thy praises!—cover'd o'er
With rosy chaplets, all my soul's desire,
　Shall centre round thy altars, while I pour

Glad songs to thee! and with the blooming maid,
　Of the deep bosom, tread the dance's maze;
Through rose-bowers fondly tendril'd by the shade
　Of mantling vines, we'll spend our summer days.

RETROSPECTIVE.

WHEN early scenes and other years,
Dim in the distant vale appears,
Fond thoughts will rush across the mind,
Which memory cannot leave behind;
These cling like ivy round the oak,
Aye fresh and green, though storms have broke
His pride, and branch'd the goodly tree,
A meditative sight to see.

All hail to thee! my native stream,
Parent of many a pleasant dream,
Where first I rudely strung my lyre,
And sung thy praise, with fond desire.
Within the rustling alder grove,
When day was spent, I loved to rove,
And trace the mellow moonlight scene,
Around thy daizy-skirted green.

Or range thy woodland banks along,
Where all around, the wakeful song
Of nature's choristers hath trill'd,
Till Vesperus their task had still'd,
And twilight's milder tints again
Were crimson'd o'er the peaceful scene;
Where—save the hum of water's fall,
Borne on the breeze, 'twas silence all.

Yes, scenes like these are ever fair,
And fresh upon the mind, though the air

We breath'd (when childhood's moody wiles
Were dimpling round our cheeks in smiles)
Hath lost that summer sunny glow,
That balm'd the valley's breast below,
And tinged each flower with richer dies,
That opened to the clear blue skies.

Yet fond remembrance paints anew
The scenes whence infancy first drew
These rude impressions, and matured
Their semblance into life, and pour'd
The living pictures as they rose,
Swelling with animation's throes,
On the heart's beating chords;—where placed,
They grew, and ne'er could be effaced.

SMILE O'ER THEM ALL.

If to grieve be a folly, then smile if you can;
To indulge melancholy, unsettles the man;
Though the ills of the world like mists hover round thee,
When sorrows are fresh, or ingratitudes wound thee,
    Smile o'er them all.

Smile if thou can, though thy eye's glaz'd and hollow,
Warm sunshine the raging tornado may follow;
Smile though thy blooming bride enters the tomb,
On the day thou would'st hail her the wife of thy home:
    Smile o'er them all!

Smile though the world wide,—all should deride thee;
Thy bosom's thy own, then rebel should it chide thee;
Smile, though despair strew the path-way before thee,
Where ruin unfurls his pale banner o'er thee:
  Smile o'er them all!

Thy smile may recall lingering hope in her flight,
When thy griefs court repose, ere she settles in night;
Kneel down at her shrine, if thy smiles she return, [spurn,
No more mourns the lorn heart,—even thee should she
  Smile o'er them all!

Thus the Muse bade me sing, saying hope is asleep,
But soon will she waken, no more must thou weep;
I see a fair sunny scene brightening around,—
Sorrow's clouds are dispelling, hope's all-cheering sound
  Whispers, smile o'er them all!

ARABELLA.

> Extinctam, omnes crudeli funere, Arabellam,
> Flebant.

SAD the mourners pace before,
 Memento Mori's, fraught with woe;
Young Arabella blooms no more,
 The pride of Gayfield-row.

Yon minute mourning-bell tolls loud;
 Its warning, thrilling knell, I know,
Strikes terror through the gazing crowd,
 Who mark death's pageant passing slow.

Her weeping mother sees the bier,
　　Borne slowly through the inquiring throng;
These wailings and that heart-wrung tear,
　　Will rankle in her bosom long.

Her gray-hair'd father bears the pall,
　　He sees not ought of all the crowd;
For hopes—fair prospects—each and all,
　　Rest with his daughter in her shroud.

Her youthful lover swells the train;—
　　What father, mother, all may feel,
Are keenly felt by him,—the pain
　　Of blighted love, who dares conceal!

The grave receives this opening flower,
　　By all who knew her, lov'd, caress'd;
Cropp'd down by thine unerring power,
　　Consumption, scourge to the human breast.

The pall's remov'd, the gilded plate
　　On the dark coffin tells thy name,
Dead Arabella! age, and date,
　　Now greets the tell-tale eye of fame.

We thought thee older than thou seem'd,
　　When Heaven reclaim'd thee as its own:
" Ætatis Seventeen!"—we deem'd
　　Thy teens were o'er, thy girlhood gone.

Thy maiden mind was premature,—
   Thy beauty, name it not—'tis gone,—
Thy worth, thy modesty so pure,
   We saw, and felt them, not alone.

The sexton as be clamp'd the sod,
   On thy bone-mingled bed of earth,
Dream'd not of Pluto's drear abode,
   Nor parents' wail, nor beauty's worth,

But carelessly some ditty sang,
   As with his spade he smooth'd the dust;
Perhaps, love never lent his pang
   To this rude misanthropist.

At pleasure now the tempest roars,
   And swirls around the cheerless lair;
While the rain-god in torrents pours,
   His watery bosom bare.

Sun, wind, or rain, she heeds them not,—
   To heaven the maiden's soul has fled,
While the mortal part, by man forgot,
   Lies mingling with its kindred dead.

Such is the tale, my brother worm!
   Rung in thine ear, from hour to hour,
And keenly felt;—still no reform,
   Till death's mandates above thee lower.

SWEET! COME AWAY MY DARLING.

Sweet! come away my darling,
   And range Rowallan glens with me;
Where balmy through the wild wood,
   Young zephyr's breath o'er flower and tree
Tells summer in her childhood
   Lies blooming all before thee;
And strews around the spangled lea,
   Full many a dainty garland.

Sweet! come away my darling,
   Rowallan woods through summer's reign,
Ne'er smiled upon a blossom,
   So peerless as the Lady Jane;—
Yon water-lily's bosom,
   Like thine's, pure without a stain,
As her snowy-cups repose them,
   On the lake's breast, my darling.

Young Fairlie and his darling,
   They wander'd down the greenwood's dell,
Where fluttering round his fond heart,
   Love panted all its fears to tell;
But hope may ward each willing art,
   And every cloud dispel,
That intervening strives to part
   Young Fairlie and his darling.

The above was suggested, after reading the following sentence
in the history and descent of the house of Rowallan: " Tradition
still points out the spot where Fairlie was married to the heiress

of Rowallan. The ceremony was performed by a curate in the fields, about a quarter of a mile from the house of Rowallan, at a tree, still called the marriage tree, which stands on the top of a steep bank, above that part of the stream, called ' Janet's Kirn.' ''

APRIL IS IN MY MARY'S FACE.

Air.—In " Tekill."

APRIL is in my Mary's face,
　　And wantons round to be caress'd,
While July in her eyes hath place,
　　Strewing young rose-buds o'er her breast.
　　　　See, glittering from the dew-clad spray,
　　　　Aurora brightens up the day,
　　　　And tells the blooming maiden May,
To garland all the wild for thee.

The hawthorn, now, the spreading sloe,
　　Shower fragrance down the vocal glen;
Where early summer glances thro',
　　The greenwood mazes once again;
　　　　I love to wander where the sound
　　　　Of falling waters aye rebound,
　　　　This fairy-haunted glen around,
If Mary tracks the world with me.

When autumn's breath has brown'd the groves,
　　The eyebright, and the asphodel,
Will linger where Pomona roves,
　　Till winter steals across the dell;

Then, Mary, will the bleak snow-storm,
Our once fair meads and glens deform;
And trackless wilds where'er we roam,
Enshrines each dear-loved scene from thee.

FAIRY MARY ANNE.

Air.—"Oh! had we some bright little isle."

When ruby-faced twilight danced over the hill,
To wake up the fairies, and weary birds still,
On the gay banks of Clutha, to meet Mary Anne,
I wander'd one evening, ere winter began.
When the breeze rustled o'er,
The wan leaves on the tree,
And strew'd all the shore,
And the sheaf-cover'd lea;
While stars twinkled bright in the firmament blue,
Reflecting their glare on the rose-drooping dew.

My bosom throbb'd quick, o'er the banks as I trod,
For I deem'd not the winds on the hill were abroad,
Till storm-chaffed clouds the pale moon overcast,
And her face was obscured in the wings of the blast.
And the stars they were gone,
As the storm gather'd round,
Yet I still wander'd on
Through the darkness profound;
For Love was my guide to the jessamine bower,
Where she promised to meet me at twilight's soft hour.

The winds died away, and the lovely moon shone
Through the bower where I plighted to make her my own;
And the fond maiden wept ere I won her consent,
The tears of affection, they flow'd and they went
    Like flowers, when the dews
      Of the night trickle there,
    Till sunbeams diffuse
      Them to perfume the air:
Now the pride of my cabin, ere summer began,
Could this heart tell its raptures, was "Fair Mary Anne!"

THE TRYSTING HOUR.

THE night-wind's Eolian breezes,
    Chase melody over the grove,
The fleecy clouds wreathing in tresses,
    Float rosy the woodlands above:
Then tarry no longer my true love,
    The stars hang their lamps in the sky,
'Tis lovely the landscape to view, love,
    When each bloom has a tear in its eye.

So stilly the evening is closing,
    Bright dew-drops are heard as they fall,
Eolian whispers reposing,
    Breathe softly, I hear my love call:
Yes! the light fairy step of my true love,
    The night breeze is wafting to me;
Over heath-bell and violet blue, love,
    Perfuming the shadowy lea.

THE SMILE OF HOPE.

ROUND the fond heart plays the smile of hope,
    When youth and love unite;
Like vernal breeze o'er new-blown flowers,
    Which court the morning's light,
When bees hum round each cup and bell,
    Meeting the raptur'd sight.

But hope can flutter round love, then die;
    Even changeful April's breath
May chill and blight the fair young flower
    She cradled on the heath,
Where the ranging bee in vain will try
    To sip new sweets from death.

I've seen the tremor on beauty's cheeks,
    Raise the lustre in her eye—
The flash wax pale—that full eye dim—
    The light smile play, then die,
And ebb on the heart; till hope recall'd
    It lipward on a sigh.

PAULONA OF MOSCOW.

WHEN we met at the altar,
    Our nuptial vows to bind,
What joy rung through the hall,
    As our willing hands were join'd;

U

And my hero bless'd the happy day,
　　When love's propitious star
Restor'd him to Paulona's arms,
　　From the red fields of war,
And bade me hope that sorrow
　　No more would cloud our mind.

Ah! fleeting were the hopes, that long
　　In secret we caress'd,
Till the larum peal'd forebodings,
　　Thrilling wild through every breast:
To arms! the trumpet sounded,
　　And my warrior sigh'd adieu!
Then hasten'd with my kinsmen
　　For the combat, while I flew
To the isles within the Kremlin,
　　Where my woes were hush'd to rest.

Hath a footstep so unhallow'd
　　Ere profaned Saint Michael's shrine!
Did a heart so steep'd in sorrows,
　　Ever court thy aid as mine,
While prostrate where thy ashes rest,
　　O patron Saint! I clung,
Calling aloud upon thee, while the yell
　　Of rapine round me rung,
When thy silver tomb, and jewel'd pall
　　I kiss'd, O saint divine!

Yes, where the frowning shadows
　　Of our Tsars were flitting around,

The infidel despoil'd thy fane,
   And dragg'd me from the ground,
Pale, shrieking to their chief,
   While his protection I implored,
And begg'd on bended knee,
   To my lorn mother to be restored,
Who mourn'd her lost Paulona,
   Weeping till she was found.

The dark and troubled waters
   Of the Moskva girdle round
Towers, battlements, and all within
   The Kremlin's hallow'd ground:
Ivan-Velikii's lofty spire,
   In gold and green surveys,
Thy princely dwellings, Moscow!
   Through the universal blaze,
Where the crimson moon frown'd o'er the wreck
   Of ruin strew'd around.

O pity! in that trying hour
   I call'd you, but ye fled;
Oblivion draw thy veil around
   The friendless orphan's head;
My Warrior, Father, Mother, long
   Will recall Paulona's woes:
She stretch'd her wan-worn lovely form
   On the spreading waste of snows,
Then closing her dark eyes, slept
   With the surrounding dead.

The foregoing Ballad was suggested upon reading the affecting story of Paulona, in Lebaume's Campaign in Russia.

" The Kremlin," says Dr. Robert Lyall in his interesting history of Russia, " if taken as a whole, with its venerable white walls, numerous battlements, variously coloured towers and steeples, present to the sight, one of the most singular, beautiful, and magnificent spectacles I ever beheld: it occupies a commanding situation on the banks of the Moskva river.

Immediately under the Cathedral of St. Michael, are the Royal Sepulchres. These are arranged in regular order under the nave, and in the trepedza of the church, defended with iron balustrades; while the tomb of St. Michael, the Patron Saint of Russia, is of beaten silver, and the pall is richly adorned with pearls and precious stones."

THE LONESOME DELL.

'Tis a dreary dell, when December's snows
Are swirling here; and the rude wind blows,
    In fitful gusty yellings round:
It is dreary still, when the woods are green,
And mantled all in summer's sheen,
    Where gule and rampion sprent the ground.

'Tis a lonesome dell—though the voice of love
Should whisper its vow in the deep green grove,
    Where the brakes 'neath the witch-elm wave;
Nae wholesome plant is e'er seen to bloom,
Where the murder'd maiden found a tomb,
    Near the bank where the Kelvin's waters lave.

'Tis a lonesome dell—for the peasants tell,
While the pear tree branch'd o'er the fountain well,
  There the struggling maiden shriek'd her last;
And his cheek grows pale, as he whispers the tale
To the stranger wandering through the vale,
  Where Kelvin waters are murmuring past.

During some passing conversation held with an old peasant, by the Pear-Tree-Well at north Woodside, upon the Kelvin, he thus addressed the visitor:—" In yonder old house (pointing eastward), some thirty-eight years ago, lived Catharine Clark with her mother. One Saturday, late in autumn, a young man, understood to be her sweetheart, called her out in the gloaming. Within two hours thereafter, he again visited her mother's cottage; the anxious mother seeing him enter alone, and also observing some spots of blood upon his hands and dress, cried out in the utmost trepidation, ' Where is my daughter?' The lad made some excuse to account for Catharine's absence, tending to lull, though not to satisfy a mother's fears; and killing a sheep were the immediate causes of her groundless fears. It was strange, that he was not immediately seized, and more so, that he was allowed to return home, to one of the low bleachfield houses down upon the river opposite Kelvin-side where he then lodged: early next morning, a search was instituted until the girl was found. She had been murdered in the hollow behind the Pear-Tree-Well, and a huge slab of granite laid over the shallow crypt wherein she lay. The Evil One must have assisted the murderer in his unhallowed task," continued the peasant, " for two stout men could with difficulty remove the stone. It also was surmisal that the wretch had fled to Ireland, as he never was apprehended for the crime."

The Pear-Tree-Well, above alluded to, is said to have received its name from a pear-tree which formerly grew over it: at present the fountain is guarded by a branching plane-tree, and two stately elms; the well which here overlooks the Kelvin in one of its most romantic scenes of wood and valley, is arched over with stone and rudely paved in front, where the thirsty pilgrim, who chooses to visit this western Arcadia of ours, and drink of its refreshing waters, will find an iron ladle, attached to a chain of the same metal, rivetted into a side stone of the fountain, bearing this memorable inscription:

" STOLEN FROM THE PEA'-TREE-WELL."

THE WINTER BOWER.

Air.—" THE ROSE-TREE."

YON winter bower is fairer,
 When moonshine's around the glade;
These glens to me are dearer
 Than balmy summer's flowery shade:
As through the pines we wander,
 Where rushes down the mountain stream
In all its native grandeur,
 Reflected o'er by Cynthia's beam.

I ranged the woodland's border,
 Where gay flowers in summer grow;
But all in wild disorder
 Lay wreathed in the drifting snow:
Yet round the bower the Christmas rose,
 And holly's scarlet berries hung,
I twined them on my love's brows,
 And kiss'd the garland blooming round.

THE SOLDIER'S RETURN.

A soldier wandering o'er the fields,
Viewing the pleasures sweet summer yields,
 Espied a maiden at close of day,
  Whilst hay was making,
She was busy raking her father's green hay.

All faint and weary he sat him down,
And eyed the maiden, whose smile had flown,
 For thoughts hung wild round her heart, whene'er
  Fond dreams recalling
Hush'd hopes that swelling, turn'd back on her dear.

O tell me, soldier! but no, she cries,
In foreign clime, my love's body lies,
 No friend wept o'er him but heaven's dew,
  O bloody Flanders!
His spirit wanders thy death-valleys through.

The soldier sigh'd as her dark eyes ran
O'er his war-worn features:—dim and wan
 Grew eye and cheek, as life's current holds
  Back on her fond heart:—
Close to his fond heart, his love he infolds.

The opening lines of the above, as well as those of the follow-ing Song, are taken from traditional Ballads, by way of rescuing from oblivion their respective airs, which are eminently beautiful, and peculiar to the Ballads themselves.

PRETTY MAID.

THERE was a pretty plough-boy,
　　A ploughing of his land,
Made his horses stand under a shade,
　　While he sang so sweet and shrill,
　　That each valley, wood, and hill,
Rung back the choral-melody:—Sweet maid!
　　　　Pretty maid!
Breezy zephyr caught the echo, Pretty maid!

By the streamlet's dimpling bosom,
　　Sat the plough-boy's blooming fair;
As his song floated up through the glade,
　　While she caught the cheering sound,
　　By young echo trill'd around,
And bade her whisper down the dell, " Your maid!
　　　　Pretty maid!
Soon will meet you by the fountain in the shade."

WELCOME SUMMER BACK AGAIN.
Air.—" HIGHLAND HARRY BACK AGAIN."

IN Flora's train the graces wait,
　　And chase rude winter from the plain;
As on she roves, the wild flowers spring,
　　And welcome summer back again:
　　　Spring dances o'er the plain,
　　　Flowering all the woodland scene;
　　　Then join with me, my lovely May,
To welcome summer back again.

The budding wild will soon perfume
  The air, when balm'd by April's rain,
'Mong banks clad o'er wi' waving broom,
  We'll welcome summer back again:
      In yon sequester'd scene,
      The mavis sings his cheerful strain,
      And there we'll meet, my lovely May,
To welcome summer back again.

When yellow cowslips scent the mead,
  Then gladness o'er the plains will reign,
And soon, my love! we'll pu' the flowers,
  And welcome summer back again:
      Spring dances o'er the plain,
      Flowering all the woodland scene,
      With blooming garlands in her train,
To welcome summer back again.

SPRING'S ANTICIPATION.

THOUGH winter o'er the hills and glens,
  In dreary wreathes reposes;
Though lone and hoary droops the briar,
  So late clad o'er with roses:
Yet soon the lovely days of spring
  Will leaf the bending grove;
Then soft the breeze will fan the air,
  And all will breathe of love.

I sat within the holly's shade,
    Bright winter's sun shone o'er me;
Glancing upon the ice-bound rill,
    That mirror'd lay before me:
No summer scene can soothe the breast,
    Like winter in her prime;
So virgin pure, her mantle floats
    Like vestal's at the shrine.

Awakening with the blackbird's call,
    The drooping snow-drop's blowing;
The cowslip, and the violets blue,
    On the gale their sweet breaths are strewing:
Oh it is sweet in glen or grove,
    To watch young spring's return,
On wind-flower bank, or crocus bed,
    Where the murmuring waters run.

DUNOON.

See the glow-worm lits her fairy lamp,
    From a beam of the rising moon;
On the heathy shore at evening fall,
    Twixt Holy-Loch, and dark Dunoon:
Her fairy lamp's pale silvery glare,
    From the dew-clad, moorland flower,
Invite my wandering footsteps there,
    At the lonely twilight hour.

When the distant beacon's revolving light
    Bids my lone steps seek the shore,
There the rush of the flow-tide's rippling wave
    Meets the dash of the fisher's oar;
And the dim-seen steam-boat's hollow sound,
    As she sea-ward tracks her way;
All else are asleep in the still calm night,
    And robed in the misty gray.

When the glow-worm lits her elfin lamp,
    And the night breeze sweeps the hill;
It's sweet, on thy rock-bound shores, Dunoon,
    To wander at fancy's will.
Eliza! with thee, in this solitude,
    Life's cares would pass away,
Like the fleecy clouds over gray Kilmun,
    At the wake of early day.

The Glow-worm (Lampyris Noctiluca) on mild summer even-ings, especially after a shower of rain, are to be found in great abundance among the long grass and moss between Dunoon and the Holy-Loch, where the surrounding scenery renders this singular insect doubly interesting. The female is larger than the male, and emits a beautiful light (apparently phosphorescent, but not really so), for the purpose of attracting the male; this issues from the four last rings of the abdomen: the male has a power of emitting a feeble light, but very disproportionate to that of the female. Two or three of these insects inclosed in a glass vase, will give a light sufficient to enable a person to read in the darkest night. There are fifty-two species of this insect scattered over the four quarters of the globe, of which two only are found in our own country, viz. the Glow-worm and the Fire-fly.

KELVIN GROVE.

LET us haste to Kelvin grove, bonnie lassie, O,
Through its mazes let us rove, bonnie lassie, O,
　　Where the rose in all her pride,
　　Paints the hollow dingle side,
Where the midnight fairies glide, bonnie lassie, O.

Let us wander by the mill, bonnie lassie, O,
To the cove beside the rill, bonnie lassie, O,
　　Where the glens rebound the call,
　　Of the roaring waters' fall,
Through the mountain's rocky hall, bonnie lassie, O.

O Kelvin banks are fair, bonnie lassie, O,
When in summer we are there, bonnie lassie, O,
　　There, the May-pink's crimson plume,
　　Throws a soft, but sweet perfume,
Round the yellow banks of broom, bonnie lassie, O.

Though I dare not call thee mine, bonnie lassie, O,
As the smile of fortune's thine, bonnie lassie, O,
　　Yet with fortune on my side,
　　I could stay thy father's pride,
And win thee for my bride, bonnie lassie, O.

But the frowns of fortune lower, bonnie lassie, O,
On thy lover at this hour, bonnie lassie, O,
　　Ere yon golden orb of day
　　Wake the warblers on the spray,
From this land I must away, bonnie lassie, O.

Then farewell to Kelvin grove, bonnie lassie, O,
And adieu to all I love, bonnie lassie, O,
  To the river winding clear,
  To the fragrant scented breer,
Even to thee of all most dear, bonnie lassie, O.

When upon a foreign shore, bonnie lassie, O,
Should I fall midst battle's roar, bonnie lassie, O,
  Then, Helen! shouldst thou hear
  Of thy lover on his bier,
To his memory shed a tear, bonnie lassie, O.

BONNIE ANN.

In summer blooms the white moss-rose,
  Pure, spotless, as the swan;
Yet peerless as celestial-rose,
  And fair, grew bonnie Ann!

When youth smiled round my yellow locks,
  Ere age had stamp'd me man;
How light the golden days wing'd on
  When near my lovely Ann!

Yes, weeping friends! when fell disease
  Through all her vitals ran;
Ye little dream'd this throbbing heart
  Beat high for bonnie Ann!

How angel-like the drooping maid,
    With face all pale and wan,
Embraced me, sigh'd, then faintly smiled—
    Adieu! said bonnie Ann!

I call'd upon my love, and wept,
    And gazed, till death began
To film her hazel eyes, then shriek'd,
    And swoon'd on sainted Ann!

The struggle's o'er!—yon chesnut showers
    His fragrance round the span,
Where rests the urn, and bends the yew
    O'er the grave of bonnie Ann.

FORTUNE'S FROLICS.

THE damsel who roams like a bee 'mongst the flowers,
    And kills with her glances each youth flitting round,
As she flaunts through the gala of morn's rosy hours,
    May be chill'd by detraction, where rivals abound:
      Ruffled flowers court decay—
      Early blown—soon away—
When fresh beauties range round in the garden of life,
      Never more will yon maid,
      Who now droops in the shade,
Be cared for or courted by you for a wife.

The debtor when stripp'd by some rogue of his all,
  'S turn'd adrift on the world, former friends seem his foes;
While the caitiff who robb'd him, smiles over his fall,
  And fattens, though drench'd from the dunghill he rose!
    Even those who were dear—
    When prosperity's ear
Only heard of your worth, nor your foibles could trace—
    Revile, slight, and shun ye,
    In misery dun ye,
When the shorn-beams of favour glance cold in your face.

SMILE THROUGH THY TEARS.

Smile through thy tears, like the blush moss-rose,
  When the warm rains fall around it;
Thy fond heart now may seek repose,
  From the rankling griefs that wound it.
For a parent's loss the eye may fill,
  And weep till the heart runs over;
But the pang is longer and deeper still,
  That wails o'er the grave of a lover.

Smile through thy tears, like the pale primrose,
  When the zephyrs play around it;
In me let thy trembling heart repose,
  I will ward the sorrows that wound it.
Ah! vain were the wish, such love to crave,
  As warmed thy maiden bosom;
Ere Henry slept, where the alders wave,
  O'er the night-shade's drooping blossom.

WELLBURN'S MARY.

I mark'd the calm on her young fair face,
  As grief's rude storm passed o'er it;
But the ebbing smile had left no trace
  Of struggles that rush'd before it.
Each grief has its day:—love weep them away,
  As the shower on April's blossom
Balms the drooping flower, till the sun's bright ray
  Drinks the tears from its virgin bosom.

The flush o'er her fair face went and came,
  As I show'd her a true-love token;
I whisper'd hope, and the young god came,
  But her virgin heart was broken!
In Wellburn garden, the white lilies bloom,
  Eke the rose round the jessamine's twining;
But they wither'd o'er Wellburn Mary's tomb,
  Ere the red winter sun there was shining.

PRINCE CHARLIE.

THOUGH bonnie raise the winter moon,
Yet weir an' strife rang wild aroun',
As Charlie an' his clans cam' down
  Frae England, o'er the border:

Their dinsom pibrochs' melody,
Brought the tear frae mony an' e'e,
To think what Charlie yet might dree,
    Wi' peril for his warder.

His diamond e'en, as black as sloes,
Were laughing o'er his Roman nose;
His cheeks like maiden-blushing rose;
    His teeth like ivory showing,
Whene'er he smiled; the prince was there
In's dimpled chin, an' brent brow fair,
An' curling locks of sandy hair,
    Beneath his bonnet flowing.

O mother! ye maun come an' see
Their tents, aboon Lord Cassel's lea;
An' tak' them what ye hae to gie,
    Afore the morning early:—
For oh! I fear hope's feeble rays,
Looks forward still on better days!
To flee before his kintra's faes,
    Can bode sma' gude to Charlie.

The above Jacobite attempt was suggested after some conversation held with a poor woman, now in the 102d year of her age. In the memorable 1745, when Charles was upon his retreat from England, he pitched his tents for two nights and a day in her neighbourhood; and the second stanza of the foregoing, describes the Chevalier's personal appearance, such as then had been impinged upon her mind, and from which description she never deviates. The fortunes of the prince, so far as they came within the scope of our centarian's observations, are sufficiently interesting, but without our province in this place.

THE SHEPHERD AND ECHO.

Dixerat, hic quis adest? Et adest, responderat echo.
Inde latet silvis, nulloque in monte videtur.—OVID.

Young echo lived within a rock,
   Alone, and far from human dwelling;
Where torrents wild the stillness broke,
   All silence from the glens dispelling.

Her wild and never-ceasing wail,
   Resounding steep, and greenwood over,
Drew a shepherd from the vale,
   Whose sighings told, he was a lover.

He sought her long through glen and dale,
   Aye she answer'd to his calling,
But never came; the rustling gale
   Drown'd her sighs in the water's falling.

She must be fair—for her voice is sweet,
   Sad—for its sounds are steep'd in sorrow:
O maiden! leave this lone retreat,
   And hie with me to the plains to-morrow.

But echo laugh'd till the welkin rung,
   And flew on the breeze the greenwood over,
While birds their sweetest warblings sung,
   Where pleased and grieved, reclined the lover.

He sought the grotto, ranged the grove,
   The sedgy brook, the winding alley;
Then sighing, call'd again, " My love!"
   " My love!"—rung back along the valley.

Like pilgrim, to the vale again
   His wandering footsteps onward bore him;
Her voice came laughing through the glen,
   Then died in breezy whispers o'er him.

'Tis a wild-goose chase!—I'll seek my home,
   And woo a maid less coy—deceiving—
While echo answer'd, " Seek my home!"
   And left the lass-lorn shepherd grieving.

BOWERDALE.

Air.—" THE YOUNG MAY MOON."

THE woodlark sang through fair Bowerdale,
His wild notes rang over wood and vale,
   But Helen, the flower,
   Left alone in the bower,
Where I parted from her, was cold and pale.
I woo'd her there, I had loved her long;
For her I had left the city's throng;
   All the world behind,
   I gave to the wind;
With Helen to live, and to love alone.

What sorrows were ours when fortune fled,
And hope's illusive dreams were dead;
  Fond feelings that rush'd
  Through my bosom, were crush'd
In their dawn, when ruin hung o'er my head—
My heart grew cold, though I feign'd to smile,
As she hung on my neck with endearing wile,
  While the sad farewell
  On my damp brow fell,
When I tore from my love and my native isle!

Through India's plains I roam'd afar,
And courted solace 'midst the strife of war:
  Yet by night or by day,
  Through danger's array,
She beam'd in my bosom hope's brightest star!
I return'd, and sought through fair Bowerdale
The friend of my love—but sorrow's wail
  Rung wild through the woods,
  O'er the dales and the floods;
For Helen, their angel, was cold and pale!

REMORSE.

Away! from the dread fascinations that flow'd,
Where the wine circled round, and the warm bosom glow'd,
With estrangement of feeling, I knew not its own,
So wildly it throbb'd, and more wild when alone:

I sought the deep grove, and the night's chilling breeze,
Where the cottage of Jessy was seen through the trees;
And vow'd soon as morning gave reason her reign,
That I never would play the wild rover again.

I wander'd unconscious that love led me there,
Till I lean'd on the oak by the blooming parterre:
O night! thou art lovely when stars twinkle bright;
But the star of my hopes met my rapturous sight
As she knelt in devotion; her orisons rose
On the whispers of night, ere she sought her repose,
While her wanderer vow'd as he paced o'er the plain,
That he never would play the wild rover again.

THE FATE OF EVELINA.

THE lava was rolling his burning flood
　　O'er the vineyards since day begun;
While the dense dark clouds threw a midnight veil
　　On the bright meridian sun!
Yon burning groves will light our way—
　　Evelina, fly!—thy loved cottage shun—
To a safe retreat, since the lamp of day
　　Is gone from our sight.　From ruin run—
　　Beloved Evelina, come!

The poison'd breeze—should its tainted breath
　　In our face blow the sulphurous air,
From the lava's tide—'twere instant death
　　To linger a moment there.
Where the palm and the olive lights the gloom,
　　And the hissing lava seeks its prey,
Vesuvius hath seal'd Resina's doom,
　　My loved one fly! we dare not stay—
　　　Beloved Evelina, come!

In vain the peasant besought his bride,
　　To flee from the mount to the plain;
But she rush'd through the burning olive grove,
　　Her loved cottage to regain:
When the lava closed, and the fire-shower fell,
　　And the earthquake shook the ground;
Still the peasant linger'd with frantic yell,
　　Calling loud through the ruins around,
　　　Beloved Evelina, come!

The catastrophe narrated here, is presumed to have taken place during the great eruption of Mount Vesuvius, in June 1794, as described by Sir William Hamilton, in the Philosophical Transactions, vol. 73; after reading his remarks made while at Rosarno, and the ruined towns around it, especially the first sentence of the following:

" The male dead were generally found under the ruins, in the attitude of struggling against the danger; but the female attitude was usually with hands clasped over their heads, as giving themselves up to despair, unless they had children near them.　In which case, they were always found clasping the children in their arms, or in some attitude or other, which indicated their anxious care to protect them.　A strong instance of the maternal tenderness of the sex."

TO LAURA.

Now the sweet scented Hare-bell,
 · Bright herald of May,
With the Pansy and Wind-flower,
   Cause woodlands look gay;
How fleeting their blossoms,
   Till the Rose has her day;
Next the Star-flowers of autumn
   Chase Rosa away.

Thus bloom and pass over,
   The pride of our year;
Each flower's called the fairest,
   Till her sisters appear:
Dear Laura, believe me,
   Thy spring, like the flowers
Now blooming, will pass away,
   Pale from our bowers.

Since morning, the Day-rose
   Smiled proudly around,
Now evening her ruby leaves
   Strew on the ground;
Then cloud not life's sunshine
   With scorns and delay,
Till thy charms, like our summer
   Flowers, all pass away.

THE DESPONDING SHEPHERD.

I ance knew content, but its smiles are awa',
   The broom blooms bonnie, an' grows sae fair;
Each tried friend forsakes me, sweet Phebe an' a',
   So I never will gae down to the broom ony mair.

How light was my step, and my heart, O how gay!
   The broom blooms bonnie, the broom blooms fair;
Till Phebe was crown'd our queen of the May,   [air.
   When the bloom o' the broom strew'd its sweets on the

She was mine when the snaw-draps hung white on the lea,
   Ere the broom bloom'd bonnie, an' grew sae fair;
Till May-day, anither wysed Phebe frae me,
   So I ne'er will gae down to the broom ony mair.

Sing, Love, thy fond promises melt like the snaw,
   When broom waves lonely, an' bleak blaws the air;
For Phebe to me now is naething ava,
   If my heart could say, "Gang to the broom nae mair."

Durst I trow that thy dreams in the night hover o'er,
   Where broom blooms bonnie, an' grows sae fair;
The swain (who, while waking, thou thinks of no more,)
   Whisp'ring, "Love, will ye gang to the broom ony mair?"

No! Fare thee well Phebe; I'm owre wae to weep,
   Or to think o' the broom growing bonnie an' fair;
Since thy heart is anither's, in death I maun sleep,
   'Neath the broom on the lea, an' the bawm sunny air.

In Johnson's "Musical Museum," we find the fragment of a repulsive legendary Ballad, with a similar burthen to that of the foregoing. There is also a traditional Ballad upon record, of which we regret our inability to procure more than the commencing stanza:—

> Ae king's dochter said to anither,
>> Broom blooms bonnie, an' grows sae fair,
> We'll gae ride like sister and brither,
>> But we'll *never* gae down to the broom *nae* mair.

Again, Sir Walter Scott causes his Effie Deans, in the "Heart of Mid-Lothian," to sing a stanza of a similar choral Ballad:

> The elfin knight sat on the brae,
>> The broom grows bonnie, the broom grows fair,
> And by there cam' lilting a lady so gay,
>> And we darna' gang down to the broom nae mair.

THE TOKEN FLOWER.

Air.—"Pretty Peg of Derby."

How bonnie is the glen in the greenwood shaw,
Where the wild roses bloom, and the breezes blaw
    Through the sunny summer dells,
    Where the woodland music swells
O'er the lily, and the bonnie blue Forget-me-not.

O tell me a flower in the garden or wild,
So modest, and so peerless, as summer's fair child;
    Not a brighter floweret blows,
    Even the blush celestial-rose,
Must yield to the bonnie blue Forget-me-not.

Y

By the cress-cover'd fountain where its sparkling waters run,
Thy azure star with golden breast is smiling to the sun,
  While the violets that bloom
   Round the fane at Beauty's tomb,
Are gemm'd with the bonnie blue Forget-me-not.

Dearest emblem of Friendship, thou beauty of the grove!
Thy pale blue eye, like my Laura's, beams with love;
  And when Laura courts the shade,
  Whisper softly to the maid,
That thy name, lovely flower! is Forget-me-not.

 Marsh Scorpion grass, the Myosotis Palustris of botanists, is a wild flower possessing uncommon beauty. This Token Flower, the Forget-me-not, is the acknowledged emblem of Friendship throughout every country of civilized Europe. Five species of this beautiful genus of plants are natives of Scotland.

CONTENTS.

JAMES HEDDERWICK AND SON, PRINTERS.